PETER HANDKE

In the same series:

Modern Literature Monographs

ooo

PETER HANDKE

Nicholas Hern

Frederick Ungar Publishing Co.
New York

First American edition 1972
© 1971 by Oswald Wolff (Publishers) Ltd.
Printed in the United States of America
Library of Congress Catalog Card Number: 76-190349
ISBN: 0-8044-2380-6

ooo

Contents

Acknowledgments

We should like to thank the following publishers for permission to use copyright material: Suhrkamp Verlag, Frankfurt/Main, for extracts from *Cries for Help, Kaspar, My Foot My Tutor*; Methuen & Co. Ltd., London, for *Offending the Audience* and *Self-Accusation*.

Chronology

arg: 81

1942: 6 December: Peter Handke is born in Griffen (in Carinthia), Austria.

1961–65: Handke studies law at the University of Graz. His first works are published in the magazine *manuskripte*.

1966: The novel *The Hornets* is published.

April: Handke attacks the Gruppe 47 in a speech at their meeting at Princeton.

June: *Offending the Audience* is premiered at the first "Experimenta" theater week in Frankfurt on the Main.

October: *Prophecy* and *Self-Accusation* are premiered together in Oberhausen.

1967: September: *Cries for Help* is premiered in Stockholm in the context of German-Swedish Theater Week.

Handke's second novel, *The Peddler*, is published.

1968: Receives the Gerhart Hauptmann Prize in Berlin. In a number of articles Handke condemns various organizations and persons (including Bertolt Brecht) for having retreated from political issues they themselves had raised.

May: *Kaspar* is simultaneously premiered in

Frankfurt and Oberhausen, and published in
Frankfurt.

1969:   January: *My Foot My Tutor* is premiered in
Frankfurt and published in the much-respected
Theater Heute.

The collection of short prose poems *The Inner
World of the Outer World of the Inner World*
is published. Handke and ten other writers set
up the cooperative publishing house Verlag der
Autoren.

1970:   January: *Quodlibet* is premiered in Basel.
Handke's third novel, *The Goalkeeper's Anxiety
at a Penalty Kick*, is published.

1971:   January: *The Ride over Lake Constance* is premiered in Berlin.

April: *Self-Accusation* and *My Foot My Tutor*
are produced at the Brooklyn Academy of Music, New York.

April-May: Handke makes a lecture tour in the
United States, speaking at several universities
throughout the country.

1972:   January: First English-language performance of
The Ride across Lake Constance is given at the
Forum, Lincoln Center, New York.

ooo

Introduction

"Boring on regardless," yawned *The Observer*. "A master wordsmith," proclaimed *The Times*. The radio critic
of each paper had just encountered the first and, until
recently, the only presentation of any of Peter Handke's
work in English. The work in question, *Self-Accusation*
(*Selbstbezichtigung*), broadcast on BBC Radio 3 in
May 1968 in a production and translation by Martin
Esslin, is probably not typical of Handke at his best.
Much more typical is the disparity of the English critical reaction, echoing as it does the reception accorded in
Germany to Handke and his work. Ever since he burst
almost simultaneously onto the literary and theatrical
scenes as recently as 1966, critics, producers and playgoers have been vociferous in their rival affirmation or
denigration of Handke's talent. The question has never
been: is he a good writer or a mediocre one? It is more
absolute than that: is he a genius or a charlatan? The
sort of question, in other words, that was asked at first
about Beckett, Brecht, Hauptmann, Ibsen, Schiller, or
Goethe, with all of whom Handke's supporters would
rank him, and indeed have done so.

True to form, each of Handke's plays regularly
causes an uproar in the theater in which it is first per-

1

formed. It is a measure of the cynicism of modern playgoers, though, that these plays then settle down to long
runs or are toured extensively, playing to audiences
many of whom seem to have come with the intention
already formed of barracking the play and heckling the
actors, rather than giving out spontaneously with
shocked retorts.

Far from being peeved at this apparent disrespect
for his brainchild, Handke appears to be inured to the
pandemonium that surrounds him. Indeed, inured is
too tame a word: he laps it up and revels in it. So much
so that from the start (that is, from his first appearance
in public as an author) critics and fellow authors were
ruefully noting a phenomenon called "Handke-Publicity" and taking sarcastic swipes at his Beatle haircut,
his effeminate features, and his championing of rock
(or "Beat," to use the German word). Since launching
himself, Handke's appearances at various functions have
usually been stormy or, at the very least, controversial,
even to the extent of his being dragged off to the police
station after a brawl outside a Frankfurt rock club. Indeed his polemical, and often politically activist essays
and speeches, the unconventional form of his theater
pieces and his whole persona are all deliberately calculated, however sincerely meant, to achieve maximum
impact on the literary and theatergoing public as well
as on the multimedia publicity machine that stands
ready to focus on anyone who makes a big enough
noise. Not that the noise of Handke's self-advertising is
anything as loud or as expert as John Lennon's, for instance (to whom, among others, Handke dedicated his
first performed play), but it is loud enough to provoke
grumbles of discontent from fellow authors who had as-
sumed their profession to be one of the least limelit in
the sphere of creative artistry.

Not for Handke, then, the slow and modest growth from sporadic critical interest in youth to unanimous acclaim in mature middle-age. Nor, it seems, the fate of the nine days' wonder. For at twenty-nine, with eight theater pieces, three novels, six radio plays, a TV play, assorted essays, short stories and prose poems, and the Gerhart Hauptmann Prize behind him, Handke can enjoy the prospect of critics and public alike eagerly anticipating his next piece and asking again the question they asked before each previous piece: Can he do it *again?*

Peter Handke was born the son of a bank clerk, on 6 December 1942 in Griffen, a small town in Austria's southernmost province, Carinthia, mountainous, forested, and studded with beautiful lakes. By his own admission, Handke grew up in the country, with the exception of a four-year interval in Berlin between the ages of two and six. These years, 1944–1948, were some of Berlin's darkest ever, but it would be foolishly fanciful to speculate on the effect the sight of the shattered city may or may not have had on the little boy. Whatever the case, it is noticeable that his writing is in fact completely clear of any trace of the harking back to the Nazi era, which so many postwar German writers have made their stock-in-trade. Handke's work is concerned solely with the present, with the reality of here and now.

From Berlin, he returned to Austria, where he went to school and, in 1961, to the University in Graz to study law for four years. Although the literary critic is often overadept at finding significance in an author's degree subject, one cannot resist drawing the inference that Handke's prose style owes much to his four years' acquaintance with statute books and the like. Most of his plays and novels consist of a series of affirmative *affirm* propositions, each contained within one sentence that is usually a simple main clause or a main clause plus one subordinate clause. The link between these sentences is not the usual one of narrative, descriptive, or psychological flow. Rather, each sentence is complete in itself and qualifies the sentence before it, or, possibly, is one of several sentences qualifying the first sentence in the chapter or section or paragraph. The effect, especially of the latter arrangement, is not unlike the series of clauses in a contract or will or lawbook shorn of linking conjunctions. It is as if a state of affairs or a particular situation were being defined and constantly redefined until the final total definition permits of no mite of ambiguity. Considering this urge toward precise definition, it is not surprising that Handke's words, like those in an insurance policy, have an exact meaning, one single interpretation. Each word has a precisely apportioned weight and contributes to the total meaning of the sentence. There are no makeweights, brought in for decorative or emotional effect. This does not result, however, in what is normally considered a spare style. Indeed, Handke has frequently been accused of self-indulgence. But it is the indulgence of repetition, not of emotional gush. It is like the action of sharpening a pencil. Each stroke of the knife achieves a greater degree of sharpness; each stroke is subtly different. But viewed quickly or disinterestedly, it looks repetitious. Handke's essays and prose pieces, on the other hand, often read more like the traditional legal document of revue sketches, where every possible contingency has been included in one gargantuan sentence, where subordinate clauses seem inexhaustible and one pants for a full stop. But the impulse is the same: to define a situation as precisely as words will allow.

Handke is well aware of the ability of this statute-book style to dehumanize, to render abstract the situation it is defining. In an essay, "I am an ivory-tower dweller" ("Ich bin ein Bewohner des Elfenbeinturms"; 1967), he describes how

Some years ago I found the law concerning martial law in a penal code: The abstract form of presentation of a ritualized death captured my imagination. The logical sequence of the sentences, which were basically all *conditional* clauses for a concrete, conceivable reality, that is, clauses that were to be used if the state of affairs specified in them occurred in reality, appeared to me utterly threatening and oppressive. They altered my previous ideas about the literary presentation of dying and death, they altered my ideas about dying and death itself. I then wrote a piece that transposed the lawbook's method into literature, and that in some sentences even consisted of the authentic legal code.

Handke goes on to say that the effect wore off when repeated, but for less sensational subject matter he has continued to use something like this technique in order to purge his writing of those emotive and self-expressive elements he so detests. This, after all, is what those who write and administer the law must strive for, too.

It was toward the end of his period at the University of Graz that one of the best Austrian little magazines, *manuskripte*, itself published from Graz, printed some of Handke's work for the first time. He had been writing short, highly structured prose pieces throughout his university career and many, dating from 1963 on, have been collected and published under the title *Salutation of the Board of Directors (Begrüßung des Aufsichtsrats)*, and subsequently republished in the Peter Handke anthology. Some of them appear to be preliminary sketches for his two novels, the first of which, *The Hornets* (*Die Hornissen*), was published the year after he left the university.

That year, 1966, was Handke's *annus mirabilis*. It started with the generally favorable critical reception of his first novel in the spring; April saw him at the twenty-eighth meeting of Gruppe 47 at Princeton, where the debut of Handke-Publicity made sure he was noticed; in June his first play stole the show at the first Frankfurt "Experimenta" theater week; by the end of the year two more plays had been premièred together at Oberhausen, and all three plays had gone straight into a paperback edition.

Handke started as he meant to go on. Gruppe 47 is a group of German writers and critics who now meet once a year to read their work and to discuss topics of literary importance. The original purpose of the group at its founding in 1947 was to try to reestablish the integrity of native German writing in the postwar period and to provide a certain safety in numbers for those eleven souls who pledged themselves to this cause at the first meeting. The list of those who had read at Gruppe 47 meetings had grown to nearly two hundred names by 1966, and the group had been meeting for nearly twenty years. It had become an established institution, and established institutions are liable to be attacked—especially by the young. And, at twenty-four, Handke was the youngest writer there. He delayed his attack until the last day of the Princeton meeting. He had already read from his second novel, *The Peddler* (*Der Hausierer*), to be published the following year. Using the ready-made format of the crime novel, it is a collection of those nonsequential, nondescriptive, single-sentence statements that have become the hallmark of

Handke's literary oeuvre. The opinion of the critics covering the meeting for the press was not favorable; it induced a "lively rigor mortis," said one. But this reaction was probably colored by Handke's subsequent outburst. Speaking from the floor, he lashed out against what he saw as the incapability of all the writers he had heard so far to write anything but descriptive prose. The effect was like reading a pictorial encyclopedia. He called this mania for literary description "trifling and idiotic," as indeed was the "superannuated criticism which accommodated itself to this kind of writing and which registered boredom at every attempt at something different." But, far from being countered with a spirited defense from one of the castigated authors or critics, this sweeping condemnation was received with beams of delight by those condemned, and the *enfant terrible* was clasped in brotherly embrace. Nevertheless, Handke had achieved his aim of getting himself and his views noticed, as he attested in a letter he wrote to *Der Spiegel*:

Ever since I was little, it has been my desire to appear in your magazine. It seemed to me that to be mentioned in *Der Spiegel* was one of the most worthwhile aims for an author to aspire to. Driven by this desire, I announced my wish to speak at the Gruppe 47 meeting, and, while I was still speaking, I could observe with delight that Herr Erich Kuby, your magazine's correspondent, was taking notes from my words. Now everything was in the bag. I made a few more strong remarks so as to be completely certain. I now conclude from Herr Kuby's report on the Gruppe 47 meeting that my stratagem has worked. I thank you very sincerely and hope that the opportunity will soon arise again for a report about me in your journal.

Indeed this outburst was to be the first of many at similar gatherings, and if people were still a little unsure of exactly what he was up to, they were to be enlightened the following June at Frankfurt.

"Experimenta I" was to be a week devoted to experimental theater that in the event included works by the established experimental playwrights Beckett and Brecht, productions by experimental theater troupes, and some brand-new experimental work by young German writers, including Bazon Brock, Otto Piene, and Peter Handke. After the relative failure of two of these pieces, Handke's *Offending the Audience* (*Publikums-beschimpfung*) succeeded in giving "the greater part of the audience one of their most enjoyable evenings for years." The hour-long piece consisted of four actors telling the audience, in a series of concise statements of fact, that they were not going to see a play that evening and that, unlike other theatrical experiences, what they were seeing had no levels of reality or significance beyond its own innate reality and significance. The actors were actors; the stage was a stage; and the audience's presence throughout was acknowledged and emphasized. The piece ended with the actors hurling insults and abuse at the audience before wishing them a cordial "Good Night."

A calculated piece of Handke effrontery, one might say, designed to gain maximum attention. Possibly, but the ideas behind it are consistent with those expressed at Princeton. Just as the mania for description is an evasion of an author's duty to come to grips with reality (a term much used and little defined by Handke), so the illusionism and symbolic trickery of the theater prevents a true presentation of this same reality. Both descriptive writing and theatrical illusionism represent a retreat into the unreal world of art.

Handke's next two plays, produced for the first

time that autumn, were bound to be a slight disappoint-
ment after the bravado of *Offending the Audience,* especially as one of them, *Prophecy* (*Weissagung*), had
been written before it. Again the audience was regaled
by four actors, who this time delivered themselves of
various prophecies of insurpassable banality such as:
flies will die like flies. The other play, *Self-Accusation,*
fulfilled the promise of its title as literally as its com-
panion piece. A man and a woman made a number of
increasingly guilt-ridden statements about their experience of life in present-day society, accusing themselves
of behavior that ran counter to the rules and expectations of that society. Both these plays were produced,
like *Offending the Audience,* on a bare stage with the
actors as actors rather than role-players. In fact, Handke
does not wish them to be called "actors" at all, but
rather "speakers," just as he refuses to call the three
pieces "plays" but rather "speaking pieces" (*Sprechstücke,* possibly on analogy with Brecht's *Lehrstücke*).

By March the following year, 1967, some ten theaters in seven countries had taken *Offending the Audience* into their repertoires, and statistics for the whole
1966/67 theater season revealed that it was the fifth
most performed play in all the German-speaking theaters of Europe, ranking it with such West End successes
as *Cactus Flower* and *The Killing of Sister George.* The
other two plays were also extensively performed and
toured to Sweden by the Oberhausen Theater, where
they were presented as part of a German-Swedish Theater Week in Stockholm in September 1967. This was
the occasion of the première of a fourth very short
"speaking piece" by Handke, called *Cries for Help* (*Hilferufe*), in which a succession of unconnected slogans,
mottoes, and catchwords, spoken by one set of actors

and countered with repeated noes from the other set, was orchestrated to lead up to a climactic ejaculation of the word "Help." Handke himself participated in the symposia held as part of the Stockholm Theater Week, his main contribution being something of a repeat of his Gruppe 47 performance—he found the whole discussion "rather annoying."

That winter he received the Gerhart Hauptmann Prize awarded annually by the Freie Volksbühne of Berlin. Neither the cash (6,000 German marks) nor the prestige that goes with it is inconsiderable. Handke acknowledged the honor with customary contrariness. He arrived late for the ceremony and delivered a militantly sarcastic speech about the acquittal of the policeman charged with the manslaughter of the Berlin student, Benno Ohnesorg. The very attempt to exclude political considerations from the trial was itself a political act, he said. Then, with ironic logic, he demanded that since there was an indisputable element of doubt in *every* accusation, all accused parties must be acquitted, and in consequence all judges, legal processes, and state institutions with power over the individual must be abolished. If Handke was snubbing the Freie Volksbühne by using their platform to make political propaganda, the Freie Volksbühne had to some extent already snubbed Handke by neglecting to retail tickets to their members for the honored prize-winner's plays. But Handke's speech was more than a slap in the face for the devilment of it (and for the publicity): it was a symptom of his growing contempt for politically orientated organizations that did not do what they said they were there to do or that retreated into aesthetics. Perhaps he considered the Freie Volksbühne to be retreating from its original obligations in this way. Certainly during the following months a number of articles came from Handke's pen condemning this or that organization or person for retreating from the political issues they themselves had raised. Among the targets were those Street Theaters founded in various German cities in 1967 and 1968 that self-consciously proclaim themselves to be Street Theaters, the Oberhausen Short Film Festival Committee, and Brecht. A motley assortment, but all the indictments are consistent.

He objects to the use made by the new Street Theaters of the irrelevant and dated techniques and subject matter of the old agitprop troupes, which makes their performances simply exercises in archaeological reconstruction. The very fact that they call themselves Street *Theaters* surrounds them with an aura of ritual, of make-believe, of *unreality*. How, then, can they make relevant revolutionary propaganda about present society and its need to be changed?

How laughable it is to look and above all to listen while people troop to the microphone one after the other, each to deliver a Brechtian *aperçu* . . . in the most cultured possible tones; and how depressing it is to listen to cabaret artists declaring the badly-needed jokes in their performances to be "Street Theater," simply because they are telling them in the open air.

The list of dos and don'ts that he then draws up for the salvation of Street Theater makes it clear that he is after something more like a shock-troop of skilled, rehearsed political demonstrators, who are expert at heckling and breaking up meetings, at leading slogan chanting, and at adding just the right sentimental appeal to revolutionary demonstrations. These tactics will work *in reality*, while anything called "theater" will be too hung up in playacting.

His objections to Brecht follow much the same lines: Brecht posed his problem—How should the world be changed?—in the theater by means of a play, which he insisted should be entertaining. He then named, or at least implied, a possible solution in Marxism. But the fact that the solution was presented in the theater, in the course of an entertaining play, meant that it remained in the realm of make-believe for the audience— it failed to make contact with *reality*. Handke writes, "I myself would support Marxism every time as the only possibility of solution . . . : but not its pronouncement in play, in the theater. . . ."

And his charge against the 1968 Oberhausen Short Film Festival Committee is a similar one of retreating behind a barrier of formalism rather than facing reality. The reality in this case was a shot of male genitals occurring in the film *Specially Commended* (*Besonders Wertvoll*) which was submitted for showing but excluded from the Festival, at which Handke was one of the jury. Handke's point is that if the subject had been treated symbolically or surrealistically or ironically it would have been accepted, "but if [the penis] is shown in one of its real functions, with a nonsymbolic hand included, one has to look on, uneasy and embarrassed, without the release of laughter or artistic appreciation of the surrealism."

It is clear that these attacks, and others like them, against what might be called a retreat from reality into formalism are consistent with his first outburst at Gruppe 47 and with his abhorrence of illusionism in the *Sprechstücke*. By asserting that his reality is the only true reality, Handke lays himself open to ridicule on all sides. This, however, he accepts with apostolic stoicism as the penalty of the true innovator and takes comfort in the tendency of literary fashion to throw up its hands in horror at each new method of representing reality (naturalism, expressionism, stream of consciousness, etc.) before eventually assimilating it to form a new norm.

The standard concept of literature labels . . . those who refuse to tell stories, who look for new methods of presenting the world and who try these out on the world as "ivory-tower dwellers," as "formalists," as "aesthetes." I will gladly let myself be labeled "ivory-tower dweller" because I believe I am looking for methods, for models of a literature that will be labeled realistic tomorrow (or the day after). . . .

But the question still remains: what *is* his way of presenting reality? It is easier to say what it is not. It rejects fiction, symbols, metaphors, even comparisons; it rejects description, illusion, subjectivity, empathy: one is left with clinical impersonality, which owes something to Alain Robbe-Grillet's implacable attempts at objectivity and more to Wittgenstein's equally implacable logic; one is left with words, which Handke entrusts with absolute meaning; and, paradoxically and unavoidably, one is left with Handke:

I don't have any themes about which I would like to write; I have only one theme: to make up my mind about myself, to get to know myself or not to get to know myself, to learn what I do wrong, what I think wrong, what I think thoughtlessly, what I say thoughtlessly, what I say automatically, what others, too, do, think, and say thoughtlessly; to become attentive and to make attentive; to make and to become more sensitive, more receptive, more precise, so that I, and others too, can exist more precisely and more sensitively, so that I can understand others better and can better associate with them.

This remarkable credo, with its deliberate overtones of John Cage's demand that we should all be "omniattentive" and of the more constructive ideals of hippie philosophy, brings back into focus the question of Handke's political commitment, raised by his Gerhart Hauptmann Prize speech. How is one to resolve the apparent contradiction between the politically revolutionary sentiments of this speech and of his blueprint for Street Theater with the apolitical nature of the ideals listed above and of his plays and novels? Why are his plays not even "committed" theater, let alone active propaganda? Partly perhaps because of his own contempt for the methods of existing "committed" literature.

It would be repugnant to me to twist my criticism of a social order into a story or to aestheticize it into a poem. I find that the most atrocious mendacity: to manipulate one's commitment into a poem or to make literature out of it, instead of just saying it out loud.

And the same applies to the theater:

Committed theater today does not happen in theaters (those falsifying art areas that void all words and movements), but in lecture halls, for instance, when the microphone is snatched away from a professor, when professors blink through burst doors, when leaflets flutter from galleries onto people assembled below. . . .

In other words, Handke is not against active commitment to a cause, but against its being carried over into and disguised as "literature." In a polemical essay, written shortly after the 1966 Gruppe 47 meeting, called "Literature Is Romantic" ("Die Literatur ist romantisch") he argues that literature and commitment are incompatible. To the committed man, defined as one who has recognized the imperfection of the existing world order and who actively desires a new one, the message is what matters, not the form in which it is expressed. Literature, on the other hand, is inseparable from the form in which it is expressed. The committed writer, then, following Sartre's call to take up his pen and show the world "as it is" and as it ought to be, is faced with an insoluble dilemma. Either he leaves the manifestoes and slogans as he finds them, in their original powerful simplicity, and neglects his duty as a writer; or he incorporates the message into a novel or rephrases it in the form of a poem and thereby rids it of its clarity, its directness, its lack of ambiguity. Even when Brecht recast genuine workers' slogans in a heightened, more rhythmical form, he formalized them into poetry and robbed them of their original reality as slogans. "Every commitment is rendered unreal by literary form. . . . The committed writer, as a writer, cannot be committed. Literature turns everything real, even commitment, into style. It makes all words unusable and corrupts them more or less." What to do then? "One can only commit oneself with actions and with words meant as actions, but not with the words of literature."

The great event of 1968 was, simply, *Kaspar*, Handke's first full-length play. In May it had a simultaneous première in Frankfurt and Oberhausen; it was subsequently produced that same year in four more German cities, including Berlin, where it was part of the Berlin Festival; it was toured by the Frankfurt Theater am Turm to the Venice Biennale; it was published by Suhrkamp Verlag and almost immediately reprinted in their paperback play series; and it was nominated "Play of the Year" by the respected magazine *Theater Heute*.

Kaspar represents a departure from the hermetic world of the *Sprechstücke*. Not that *Kaspar* is a drawing-room comedy or even Brechtian parable, although it is perhaps nearer the latter than Handke might care to admit. Onto a stage littered haphazardly with items of furniture steps, or rather staggers, Kaspar, a clownish figure who can hardly walk and who can utter only one sentence, which he does repeatedly and indiscriminately. During the first half of the play this figure learns, or is taught, to speak, to name things around him, and to put his immediate surroundings in order. His teachers are disembodied voices that come through loudspeakers. They then instruct him in various model precepts, and by the end of the first half Kaspar appears to be a fully integrated member of society. In the second half, against a background of a crescendo of cacophonous noises made by several other (identical) Kaspars, the original Kaspar reminisces about events in the first half and emphasizes his new self-awareness and integration with his surroundings. Finally Kaspar loses coherence, so that he is only able to say: "I am I only by chance."

October 1968 saw another new departure for Handke with the broadcast by West German Radio, Cologne, of his first radio play, called simply *Radio Play* (*Hörspiel*). Five more radio plays and a play for television were to follow in the next two years.

And the following year Handke succeeded in astonishing both his admirers and detractors with the first performance of a new play in which two characters appear but not a word is spoken throughout the length of the play. This from the author of the *Sprechstücke*, which consisted of *nothing but* words! The play, produced in January at the Frankfurt Theater am Turm by Claus Peymann, who had been responsible for two earlier Handke premières (*Offending the Audience* and *Kaspar*), has as its title *My Foot My Tutor* (*Das Mündel will Vormund sein*). In ten scenes, the two characters perform various ordinary and not so ordinary actions in and around a sparsely furnished farmhouse. The actions range from eating an apple and reading a paper to throwing bottles and plates, and all serve to demonstrate, without the necessity for speech, the relationship between the two men. It is that of guardian to ward, of dominant to subservient. The play was published that same month in *Theater Heute* and republished later in the year in the Peter Handke anthology.

In the spring of 1969 another new work made its appearance, in the Suhrkamp paperback series. *The Inner World of the Outer World of the Inner World* (*Die Innenwelt der Außenwelt der Innenwelt*) is the cryptic title of a collection of forty-two short prose poems written between 1965 and 1968. One or two of the most intriguing pieces are what can only be called "literary ready-mades," such as the cast and credits for the film *Bonnie and Clyde* or the Japanese Top Twenty for 25 May 1968 reprinted without alteration or comment.

Two further publications in 1969 indicated conclusively how far Handke had come in three short years in terms both of critical esteem and of popular impact. One was the autumn number of a German critical quarterly devoted exclusively to an appraisal of Handke by several eminent critics. The quarterly, *Text und Kritik*, had hitherto featured similar appraisals of such figures as Robert Musil, Georg Trakl, Heinrich Heine, Ezra Pound, and Henry James! In fact the editor reports that Handke's own first reaction to the projected volume

was "Perhaps this Handke-number is one of your jokes."
Not the least interesting item is a select bibliography of
books and articles on Handke published between March
1966 and July 1969: it occupies more than nine double-
columned pages.

The second, more popular publication was a 365-
page volume referred to by the publishers as a "Peter
Handke Reader," and containing reprints of most of his
prose pieces, some of his poems, twelve essays culled
from various magazines, the plays *Offending the Audience* and *My Foot My Tutor*, and a first publishing of
Radio-Play No. 2 (*Hörspiel Nr. 2*). It is almost a collected edition of his works. The amount of reprinted
material makes it clear that the publishers were not aim-
ing at Handke devotees but at a new public who might
have been skeptical hitherto. The first printing of this
moderately priced volume (12.80 German marks) ran
at fifteen thousand copies, in marked contrast to the
first print order of three thousand for his first novel.
Meanwhile, the paperback *Sprechstücke* was nudging
one hundred thousand. These are not, of course, best-
seller figures, but they are remarkable for an author who
is still labeled "avant-garde," "experimental," "difficult."

These two seals of approval gave credence to the
suspicion that Handke was almost becoming respect-
able, albeit on his own terms. The Princeton-style out-
bursts were a thing of the past, and the frequency and
contrariness of his pamphleteering seemed to be abat-
ing. Business investment was a logical next step: toward
the end of 1969, Handke and ten like-minded writers
set up a cooperative publishing house, Verlag der Autoren, whose list soon boasted successful plays by many of
the new young playwrights who had benefited from the
more liberal atmosphere created in some measure by

Handke's frontal assault on the conventions of theater: Bazon Brock, Rainer Werner Fassbinder, Dieter Forte, Heinrich Henkel, Harald Sommer, Martin Sperr, Jochen Ziem.

The year 1970 saw an enthusiastic but respectful reception of his third novel, *The Goalkeeper's Anxiety at a Penalty Kick* (*Die Angst des Tormanns beim Elfmeter*), a lightly Kafkaesque detective story in which the main concern is the nature of the fear felt by a murderer, in this case an exgoalkeeper. And when Handke's seventh stage play, *Quodlibet*, premièred at Basle in January in an improbable double bill with an early Lessing play, failed to arouse audience or critics to excitement of any kind, Handke contented himself with a brief and calmly worded postscript in the April *Theater Heute*. Perhaps he realized the play was hardly worth campaigning for, when even the gifted and usually controversial director, Hans Hollmann, had been unable to inspire the short play's feeble audience-gulling tactics with much life.

Handke's theatrical reputation was rapidly restored the following season when a particularly impressive new interpretation of *My Foot My Tutor* joined the list of successful Handke productions at the Berlin Forum-Theater, which had already given two hundred twenty-five performances of *Kaspar* and five hundred of *Offending the Audience*. And in January 1971, his second full-length play, *The Ride over Lake Constance* (*Der Ritt über den Bodensee*), was playing to ninety-nine percent houses at the progressive Schaubühne am Halleschen Ufer, Berlin, whose politically conscious directors had presumably sensed the fundamental criticism of society that lies at the heart of this phantasmagoric but hugely entertaining play.

With this play Handke proved once more that he *could* still invent a valid form of theater without resorting to the despised conventions of plot, character, and dramatic construction. He continues to amaze his critics, but their amazement is still compounded of an element of defiance. Handke is constantly "dared" to bring off the impossible with each new play; and he has risen to the challenge and transcended it. For despite the pyrotechnics of his experiments with form, he has succeeded in constructing a consistent *Weltanschauung* that has defined itself more clearly with each new play. It is the aim of this study, which can only be in the nature of an interim report, to examine the stages of construction.

1

ooooooooooooooooooooooooooooooooooooooooooooo

Offending
the
Audience

The text of this play is prefaced by a short list of seventeen "Rules for the Actors." (This is the only time Handke uses the word "actor" in connection with his *Sprechstücke;* otherwise they are speakers. The casting for this play is simply "Four speakers.") These rules are a series of "look and listen and learn" instructions, directing the actors' attention to various more or less mundane sights and sounds, to be heard emanating from Catholic churches, football crowds, riots, debates, simultaneous translation systems, bicycle wheels, cement mixers, trains, the Rolling Stones, and the Radio Luxembourg Hit Parade, and to be seen demonstrated by loiterers, animals at the zoo, Lee J. Cobb, Gary Cooper, and the Beatles. Just as John Cage insists that all sound is music, and Ann Halprin that all movement is dance, so Handke seems to be saying to his actors that the very mundanity of these visual and aural experiences should not invalidate them. They are worth seeing and worth hearing for their own sake and Handke even emphasizes certain parts of each experience as particularly noteworthy: for instance, the gradually increasing noise a cement mixer makes when it has just been turned on. By forcing his actors' attention on these underestimated sights and sounds, Handke presumably wishes them to make use of their increased sensibility in the acting of his play and, in turn, to make the audience more aware of the richness of the ordinary world around them. This would tally with the final sentence of Handke's "Note to My *Sprechstücke,*" where he says that his *Sprechstücke* are not intended to "revolutionize, but to make aware." And this in turn tallies with John Cage's philosophy, shared by many artists engaged in Happenings and similar events, that we should all be "omniattentive."

On a more practical level, it would be possible to

incorporate the insights gained by following the instructions in the active presentation of the play. In a play
with no specific movement, no role-playing, no scenery,
and no illusion, speech is obviously at a premium, as
Handke intends it to be. It will obviate monotony and
will lend force to the words if they are orchestrated into
interesting and variegated patterns. Many of the sounds
cited by Handke, such as the chanting of slogans in a
riot, the response in a litany, the interruptions in a de-
bate, the clicking of a freewheeling bicycle as it comes
to rest, or the driving beat of a Rolling Stones number,
could clearly provide models for just such speech orchestration, often lending extra meaning to the words
spoken (as, for instance, any phrase when chanted to an
accelerating rhythm carries excitement whatever its literal meaning). These, though, are the lessons taught by
Antonin Artaud and effectively practiced by his disci-
ples, Peter Brook, The Living Theater, and others. They
should be within the ken of most actors and certainly
of all modern directors.

More to the point are references to rock music,
which Handke has elaborated on elsewhere: "I wanted
to communicate to others the effect of 'beat' music on
me—and it was a revolutionary effect—by creating with
words and phrases a structurally similar effect. . . ."
More recently in an interview with Artur Joseph,
Handke has qualified this statement:

I adopted structures that were particularly noticeable in
beat. They exist all over the place, in noises or sequences
of sound. . . . I had noticed that a frequent bravura
phrase in beat is a quite particular sound sequence that
one can describe pictorially like this: a train starts out of
the station, gradually leaves the station, becoming softer

and softer. And at the same moment a second train pulls
in becoming louder and louder. And finally it stops dead.
This structure, these simple sequences, are often used in
beat. A very fast variation of rhythmic patterns is running
on and there suddenly comes a break—these patterns go on
in a completely different tempo. It is not only in beat one
can find this sort of thing, but it is there it becomes quite
distinct, and it is there that it attracted my attention.

The first and several subsequent producers of the
play, however, have not confined themselves solely to
these considerations of speech orchestration. By prepar-
ing a script devoid of stage directions, Handke obviously
laid himself open to "free interpretation," possibly a result of his lack of theatrical experience, which, however,
he has rapidly gained, so that in his later plays every
twitch of the eyebrow is accounted for. Consequently,
the first production saw the actors relying "less on beat
rhythms and more on the tried and tested theatrical me-
dia such as mime, intonation, and choreography. . . .
They stood, knelt, lay, and spoke over the footlights, in
the auditorium, from the wings, and on the empty stage
(flats stacked haphazardly back to front against the
back wall); they crawled into the prompter's box; they
carried the lid of the prompter's box around with them;
once, almost as if in a farce, their heads appeared round
the left side of the stage one above the other." But
Handke has subsequently complained that

The play was pepped up out of fear that the audience
would perhaps be wearied by the continuous speaking. Of
course one must speak the play, but one does not need to
stand motionless on the stage; one can walk around, move
about casually. But nevertheless hold the audience's attention by changes in the rhythms of speech. There is such an
infinite number of possible tempos of speech that one can

always draw the audience into the spell so that they listen just because they are curious as to what is coming next.

This last remark—"they are curious as to what is coming next"—explains the care that the author has lavished on the introductory passage that precedes the play proper. A set of extremely detailed instructions explain how, long before the curtain goes up, the theater should be prepared for the elaborate practical joke that is to be played on the unsuspecting audience. Like all practical jokes it only really works on unsuspecting people, and this is a charge that can be leveled against the whole play, that it is a "once-off" joke that does not bear repetition to those who know it.

This preamble is a thematic foreshadowing of the play itself in another, more important way. Handke desires that, from the moment the audience enters the theater (or, indeed, is turned away for being too informally dressed), the house manager and his staff shall make every effort to maintain and even slightly heighten the usual ritual associated in the audience's mind with going to the theater. The cooperation of the stage manager is sought in having certain noises and movements made behind the curtain so as to whet the audience's appetite for the coming show. And then, after a particularly slow and suspenseful dimming of the house lights, the curtain goes up and—surprise, surprise!—the stage is totally bare, and on it are four ordinarily dressed people who are apparently rehearsing. The stage is lighted by the same even light that illuminates the auditorium.

What has happened is that the mumbo-jumbo surrounding conventional theatergoing has been set up with the deliberate intention of knocking it flying by a display of *un*conventional theatrical goings-on that negate most of the audience's conventional expectations.

The audience has been "had," and, as if thumbing a
nose, the four people on the bare stage are rehearsing a
crescendo of insults. This pattern, of the audience having their theatrical expectations foiled and then being
insulted, is precisely the pattern of the play itself.

The play on the page consists of sixty-six paragraphs of varying lengths, which are neither ascribed to
particular speakers nor grouped in any way. During the
course of the play Handke has his speakers tell the audience: "You have recognized the dialectical structure
of this play," by which is meant that attention is alternately focused on the audience and the actors, or on the
worlds each inhabits.

The progression of the play can be said to be spiral.
Most of the main themes are stated simply within the
first few paragraphs, and these are then reiterated and
elaborated in turn perhaps three or four times during
the play. These themes include the fact that the play is
a prologue, which is later elaborated to mean a prologue
to, among other things, the audience's future theatergoing; that the play is not a conventional play of any
known type, there is no acting, no spectacle, and no
storytelling; that the audience's theatrical expectations
will not be satisfied; that the audience is an orderly
group of people who are experiencing certain sensations
and thinking certain thoughts; that, because there is no
difference between the world experienced by the people
on stage and the world experienced by the people in the
auditorium, actors and audience can be said to form an
undivided unity; that the dimension of time in particular is identical on stage and in the auditorium, as it
elapses at the same rate in both areas; that there is no
symbolic level to the play or to anything on stage, because everything is what it is in reality and nothing

more; that there is no theatrical illusionism or trickery; and that the _audience_ is the central theme of the evening's entertainment.

These reiterated points build to a passage about two-thirds of the way through the play (the classic position for a dramatic climax) that consists of a frontal assault on the sort of play the audience has supposedly been used to watching hitherto. The passage is marked out from the rest of the play by its reference to past events while the rest of the play is concerned only with the present, by its more coherent and sequent argument, and by its variegated sentence structure in contrast to the protracted anaphora of most of the play. The object of the onslaught is the dead theater of pretense and illusion, where things were never what they seemed but something else as well. In favorable contrast to this double-natured nonsense is mentioned "the pure play," which is defined as being "timeless" or having the same dimension of time as exists in real life and not a false, make-believe time. In this attack is clearly discernible the voice of the upstart at Princeton and subsequent campaigns on all fronts against fictions, metaphors, and illusion. Indeed this passage is an epitome of the action of the whole play. Having physically demonstrated the exclusion of all the usual fictive theatrical devices, the actors complete the purification process with an explicit verbal attack on the old forms.

The rest of the play is a sort of coda. First comes a final restatement that this play has none of the conventional trappings of role-playing, simulated action, symbolic levels of meaning. Then the actors explain how the audience will leave the theater and make their different ways home. "Before that, however, you are going to be insulted." There follows the most notorious section of the play, the section that gives the play its title. And yet it doesn't consist solely of abuse aimed at the audience. The insults are alternated with extravagant praise for the "performance" the audience has just given. These accolades, which at first far outweigh the abuse and only gradually give way to it, are the sort of clichés used by drama critics to praise naturalistic performances. Throughout the play the actors have been ever more insistent that, since there is no distinction between stage and auditorium, the audience has been giving as much of a performance as the actors: and now critical cant, such as "You were lifelike. . . . You *lived* your parts. . . . You were the ideal cast," when applied to the audience, who could hardly help being lifelike, succeeds in casting another ironic slur on the whole business of conventional role-playing. The insults themselves are increasingly polysyllabic, increasingly noninsulting, and often witty, both individually and because of their fantastic profusion (one hundred and sixty-four of them).

The play ends with the actors thanking the audience and wishing them good-night. The curtain falls but is immediately raised again to reveal the actors standing looking expressionlessly into the auditorium. A deafening sound of wild applause comes over the loudspeakers and continues until the audience leaves. Then the curtain comes down.

It is not surprising that this play was immediately dubbed an "antiplay" and Handke's form of theater "antitheater" (a label that Handke himself has rejected). Comparisons were made with the famous self-named "antiplay" of the previous generation, Ionesco's *Bald Prima Donna.* But it is important to be clear that in these cases (as also with *Ubu Roi,* the daddy of modern antiplays) the "anti" is only relative to what has gone before: none of these antiplays represented an act of total destruction, because each of them could only exist and could only make sense within the structure of the existing theater against which it was rebelling. *Offending the Audience* is a playgoer's play, and far from being anti, it depends on the theater as an institution.

The play is also dependent on a number of well-tried theatrical devices. Surprising the audience and deceiving their expectations is one of the oldest. Direct address is as old as the Greeks or medieval religious plays and as modern as Brecht. Making the audience part of the performance is as old as the court masques and as new as the Happening. There *is* even a degree of role-playing despite the constant disclaimers. Statements such as "We have no roles. We are ourselves. We are the mouthpiece of the author" reveal niceties of distinction between illusion and reality that outdo Pirandello. Nevertheless, like the actors in *Six Characters in Search of an Author*, Handke's actors *are* actors acting actors and not the ordinary people they are required by the author to say they are. But these are fine points, and it is true to say that, for all the theatricality of the play, Handke has done away with a prodigious number of what are normally considered necessary ingredients for a theatrical piece. For this reason, the same ground could hardly be covered again in subsequent plays. Rather like the minimal painter who has reduced his art to a bare canvas, Handke reached a dead end with his first play and had to strike out in a new direction. Nevertheless, the play can be seen as a necessary cleansing procedure, a wiping of the slate prior to a new set of inscriptions; hence, perhaps, the insistence that the play is a prologue—a prologue to his own subsequent plays.

As well as sharing the misused label of antiplay, *Offending the Audience* shows other remarkable similarities of origin and structure with *The Bald Prima Donna*. According to Martin Esslin in *The Theatre of the Absurd*, Ionesco's play had originally ended quite differently from the present version:

Ionesco had planned to let the maid, at the height of the quarrel, announce "The Author!" after which the author would appear, the actors would respectfully step aside and applaud him while the author would approach the footlights with sprightly steps, but suddenly raise his fists and shout at the audience, "You bunch of crooks! I'll get you!"

The similarity between this and the end of *Offending the Audience* is hardly mere coincidence. Both are born of a distrust, almost a hatred, of conventional theater and of the audience that patronized it. Ionesco has described his attitude to the theater at the time he wrote the play:

For me, going to a public performance meant going to see apparently serious people making a public exhibition of themselves . . . what worried me in the theater was the presence of characters in flesh and blood on the stage. Their physical presence destroyed the imaginative illusion. It was as though there were two planes of reality, . . . two antagonistic worlds failing to come together and unite.

And it was an uncomfortable awareness of "two planes of reality" in the theater that similarly spurred Handke to write his first play. The difference being that Handke had no respect for the fictional or imaginative plane and wished to see it abolished.

He wrote: "The theater as it was was for me a relic from a past era. Even Beckett and Brecht had nothing to do with me. Stories on the stage did not work for me;

instead of being simple, they were always only simplifications. The possibilities of reality were limited by the impossibilities of the stage. . . ." Like Ionesco, Handke too experienced initial dislike of the theater:

On one occasion I arrived at the theater too late, and while I waited in the foyer, I heard, behind the closed doors, the actors acting reality: *what* they were performing I didn't understand, but I heard the tense, quiet, irritated, casually spoken, muffled, mocking, subdued, reflective, soundless sounds; that was good enough, but it hasn't been sufficiently provoking for me to be able to deduce my aversion to the theater from it alone. I have an aversion, that is clear; I had aversions before I wrote the play *Offending the Audience*, and I tried to put something rational, words, in the place of aversions precisely by writing the play.

In fact, he first thought of writing not a play but an essay, "a pamphlet against the theater, but then I recognized that a booklet is not the right place to publish attacks on the theater. It would probably have been ineffective. And so arose the paradox of doing something in the theater against the theater, of using the theater to protest against the current theater. . . ."

Handke and, equally, Ionesco are not of course alone in their discovery of the impact of using the theater against the theater. The dadaists in Zurich and Paris during and immediately after World War I had, as usual, done it all before. Their soirées, or, as we might now call them, mixed-media events, were considerably more destructive in intent and more relentlessly opposed to all the recognized canons and categories of art than Handke's or Ionesco's vigorous but comparatively stylish protests. Handke has also invited comparison with the dadaists on account of his successful self-advertisement, but again there is a constructive purpose and ultimately a restraint that does not accord with dadaist nihilism. In this respect Handke rather resembles the modern purveyors of Happenings and other crypto-theatrical events, who are often labeled neo-dadaists. The resemblance is not great and is too easily misleading, but, as far as it goes, both turn their backs on conventional theater while using basic theatrical devices to give their audiences a new and more immediate contact with reality. The Happening aims to achieve this by the audience's total or partial participations in the event, with a resultant variability in the nature of that event; while, despite the variable element of heckling from the audience (which Handke seems to enjoy), *Offending the Audience* usually adheres closely to the shape given it by the author.

A much nearer resemblance to Handke's play is borne by some of the work of the Vienna Group, five young experimental writers (Konrad Bayer, H. C. Artmann, Gerhard Rühm, Oswald Wiener, Friedrich Achleitner) who worked together for about ten years beginning in 1952. As Handke's compatriots and contemporaries, their work and possibly some of the writers themselves were known to him, and his own work now appears in little magazines alongside that of exmembers of the Group. Konrad Bayer, their spokesman, writing in 1964, labeled Rühm and Achleitner "concrete poets" who "aimed at constructive, materially-orientated writing (harking back to expressionism and the Bauhaus, drawing inspiration from Wittgenstein's writings . . .)"; and Bayer was particularly interesting on the subject of "our contributions to a possible theater of the future— presented under the guise of cabaret sketches . . . (1958, 1959: demonstrations of 'facts,' public acts of destruction, exercises in awareness, attempts at total theater)." Even from these slight descriptions the shared concerns of both Handke and the Vienna Group are apparent. Handke's theater, too, is interested in the presentation of facts rather than fictions; as for awareness, Handke has said his *Sprechstücke* aim to "make aware"; and his writing, too, is "materially-orientated" and influenced by Ludwig Wittgenstein, though Handke is not a "concrete" writer in the generally accepted sense of that term. It is also clear that the Vienna Group has learned from dada and has something in common with the Happening ("public acts of destruction," etc.).

One of Bayer's published ideas for a theatrical event (it forms a section of *der stein der weisen*, Berlin, 1963) illustrates some of the concerns shared with Handke:

i will write a play with the title: *the sun burns*. then i will find a building or have one put up that conceals in its ground floor or cellar a space suitably large to be partitioned by a curtain into 2 auditoria, each to take about half of all the people. they sit there and look at the curtain from each side . . . each of the two compartments has its own access . . . each of these sections of the space separated by the curtain is a theater. each of these two theaters has its own box office at its own entrance. in both theaters the first performance of my play with the title *the sun burns* is being got ready. both theaters open at the same time. a flood of publicity is essential. both announce the première of the play *the sun burns*. the human race sits assembled. the curtain goes up. both halves of all the people stare each other in the face. with that the play *the sun burns* is written.

This piece is undoubtedly funnier in the telling than in any possible execution of the idea. Nevertheless,

if one imagines it duly carried out, the effect on the audience of this piece would be strikingly similar to the
effect of Handke's *Offending the Audience*. By being
confronted by another audience where it was expecting
a play, Bayer's audiences would be made uncomfortably
aware of the state of being an audience, which exactly
tallies with Handke's speakers' nagging insistence that:

By the fact that we speak to you, you can become aware of
yourselves. Because we address you, you gain in self-
awareness. You become aware that you are sitting. You
become aware that you are sitting in a theater.

Both Handke's and Bayer's strategems could be seen as
extensions of the Brechtian desire to prevent the audience from falling willing victims to the hypnotizing illusionism of the theater by jerking them back into reality so that they are better able, mentally and spiritually,
to deal with the issues raised on stage. Indeed, this is a
large part of Handke's avowed purpose, except that he
would extend the process to the audience's being better
able to deal with life as well:

The play has not been written so that the usual audience
should make way for a different audience, but that the
usual audience should become a different audience. The
play can serve to make the spectator pleasantly or unpleas-
antly aware of his presence, to make him aware of himself.
It can make him aware that he is there, that he is present,
that he exists. . . . It can make him attentive, keen of
hearing, clear-sighted, and not only as a playgoer.

If Bayer's piece is anything more than a "public act
of destruction" (destruction in this case of an audience's
expectations), it is about what Handke's play is about:
something that might grandly be called the nature of

reality in the theater. The point that both pieces make
is that in the theater, where fantasy, illusion, make-
believe, and fiction—in a word, unreality—are the order
of the day, one of the few *real* elements in the theatrical experience is the audience.

Unlike other theatrical revolutionaries anxious to
change the role of the audience in the theater, Handke
does not worship at the shrine of audience participation.
When members of The Living Theater leave the stage
in *Antigone* to scream filthy abuse at the audience, it is
not at all the same thing as the 164 scripted insults with
which Handke's speakers regale their audience. The
Living Theater and their imitators wish to draw the audience into the vortex of the play by extending emotional involvement beyond the confines of the stage into
the auditorium; Handke on the other hand wishes his
audience to remain supremely aloof and in control of
themselves so that they may resist the feigned yet hyp-
notic emotional lure of the stage action. The Living
Theater's insults intend to merge actor and audience:
Handke insults his audience so as to remind them that
they *are* audience.

Offending the Audience, then, is a theatrical event
that has done away with almost all of the normal ingredients of theater, such as plot, character, theatrical time,
place and action, and even perhaps mimesis or role-
playing. It even manages to throw doubt on one of the
most accommodating definitions of theater in existence:
"A impersonates B while C looks on" (Eric Bentley).
What remains is a stage, an auditorium, some people
who speak, and others who spectate. The speech is used
to underline what is already obvious: that most of the
elements of conventional theater are deliberately miss-
ing but that there is going to be no attempt to form a

play or anything normally accepted as theater from what is left.

What is exciting and entertaining is both the thoroughness with which this one basic idea of nontheatricality is executed and, complementary to that, the inventiveness with which such thin gruel is made sustaining for thirty pages of text or sixty minutes of performance. It is a very theatrical nontheatricality. It is even frequently witty, for instance in the juxtapositions of the anaphora and in the novelty and variety of the final orgy of abuse.

By depriving his own piece of most of the trappings of conventional theater and yet producing a viable theatrical event, Handke both acts out his wish to destroy the despised mechanisms of plot and character, illusion and make-believe, and also demonstrates the feasibility of dispensing with them, confining himself instead to the true reality of here and now, the reality in which the audience exists. For the audience is the hope for the future; by making the audience constantly aware of themselves in the theater, he hopes to make them repudiate the old brand of theatrical unreality and accept only their own reality. Having changed them, having opened their eyes to a new awareness, he considers them ready for a new kind of theater. *Offending the Audience* is after all "a prologue"—that is, a prologue to, among other things, Handke's subsequent plays.

2

Prophecy

In the "Note to My *Sprechstücke*," Handke says: "The *Sprechstücke* make use of the natural expressive form of abuse, of self-accusation, of confession, of assertion, of query, of justification, of excuse, of prophecy, of cries for help." It will be noticed that the titles of all four *Sprechstücke* are drawn from this list. (The more literal translation of *Publikumsbeschimpfung* is *Abusing the Audience*.) *Prophecy* is one of them. Like the other *Sprechstücke*, it is halfway toward being a "pure play": it has no characters, no plot, no illusionism; it exists in the same stratum of time and on the same plane of reality as does the audience.

It is probably fair to say that *Prophecy* is one of those pieces that would never have seen the light of day without the success of later work by the same author, for *Prophecy* was actually written before *Offending the Audience* but performed after it. Indeed, it is problematical whether it was first conceived for performance at all. Unlike *Offending the Audience*, it can gain no genuine extra dimension in the theater. For although a director might trick out a production with movement, effects, and rhythmic delivery, he would be unlikely to add anything to the meaning of the piece, whereas, in a very real sense, *Offending the Audience* does not exist without an audience.

In its published form, *Prophecy* consists of thirteen pages of script and a "cast list" of "Four speakers (a, b, c, d)." The script is made up entirely of autonomous simple sentences, each of which is written on a separate line, and most of which include an adverbial phrase beginning "like. . . ." The sentences are grouped into "speeches," most of them only single sentences, but one as much as fifteen. The "speeches" are allotted in rotation either to individual speakers (a, b, c, d) or to combination of speakers (ab, abc, abcd) or both (d, ad, b, c, b, abcd). Since there is no thematic correlation between the separate speeches given to any one speaker, the intention must be to form abstract patterns of single and unisonous voices.

The trouble is that this bears no relation to the actual meaning of the sentences, which are a series of statements of the obvious, created by comparing a phenomenon with itself. Thus: "Statues will stand like statues" or "Blood will be red like blood" or "Those struck by lightning will fall as if struck by lightning" or "Ashes will burn to ashes" or "Chalk will be chalk white." (These five examples represent the five grammatical patterns that are variated to form other statements.) All the sentences are cast in the future tense, giving them, as the title suggests, a prophetic ring not unlike the more incantatory passages of Isaiah or Revelation, with the anaphoric "And" and "But" deliberately increasing the resemblance.

But what is it all about? A clue may be found in the five-line epigraph quoted from a poem by Ossip Mandelstamm, a member of the Russian Acmeist circle, who reacted against the impressionism and mysticism of the symbolists in favor of conciseness and concrete imagery. The lines read:

> Where to begin?
> Everything cracks in its joints and totters.
> The air shudders with similes.
> No word is better than the other,
> The earth resounds with metaphors. . . .

This apocalyptic vision of a world bombarded with metaphors and similes, infected with a passion for describing everything as or like something else emphasizes the problem facing the writer who simply wants to describe things *as they are*, without recourse to resemblances and comparisons. This one recognizes as Handke's problem, too, and he has said as much in an essay called "Theater and Film: The Misery of Comparison" ("Theater und Film: Das Elend des Vergleichens"):

> Pascal said something like: the whole misery stems from the fact that people insist on believing that they must compare themselves with infinity. And another misery— which Pascal did not mention—stems from the fact that people believe that they must make comparisons *at all*. . . . How does this mania for making comparisons arise? . . . Does it not come about from our incapacity to differentiate individual entities? And how does it arise that in making comparisons one always wants to make value judgements at the same time? Is it not true that one makes value judgements because one is incapable of first perceiving the . . . object at all?

Handke's reaction to this state of affairs is to devalue the simile construction industry by taking it to its logical conclusion, in an effort to restore the powers of simple perception to himself and to his audience. By comparing each phenomenon with itself rather than with something alien to it, he throws the emphasis back onto the individuality, the *reality* of the phenomenon itself. A rose is a rose is a rose.

Handke's problem in *Prophecy* is to restore to this type of self-evident truth the freshness of its original impact. It was a problem he had faced with his first novel, *The Peddler*, which was written deliberately using the stereotyped forms and format of the crime novel:

> It was not concerned with "unmasking" clichés (they are perceptible to anybody with a modicum of sensibility) but,

with the help of clichés drawn from reality, to come to new conclusions about (my) reality: to make a method productive again that was already automatically reproducible.

This could be said to be his aim in *Prophecy*, too. And in this, one can see again the Handke of Princeton and *Offending the Audience* striving to open the eyes of his audience to the true reality that underlies false layers of fiction and figures of speech. Unfortunately the verdict of most critics was that, in *Prophecy*, he failed to do so.

3

Self-Accusation

"Using the theater as a moral institution gets on my nerves," Handke told Artur Joseph, but went on to qualify this a moment later:

Insofar as theater makes people aware that the authority that one person wields over another can operate in ways that people were previously ignorant of, that people had accepted as customary—if these suddenly appear to people as artificial, as not at all natural, and indeed [if this is done] by means of the theater, by means of a linguistic disclosure, by means of grammatical deductions, which suddenly show people that the way domination is effected is neither divine nor statutory, then the theater can be a moral institution.

It would seem to be these conditions that Handke is attempting to fulfill in *Self-Accusation*. And the concern with the functioning of authority and the ways in which one person dominates another marks the emergence of a new theme in his plays. It is a concern that should not surprise anyone who bears in mind the other side of Handke's public persona—the political activist. It is a theme that he takes up again, more fully, in *Kaspar* and *My Foot My Tutor*. For *Self-Accusation*, however, the limitations of the *Sprechstücke* remain, limitations that Handke is ironically aware of:

At first I had planned a play with a genuine action, with a story, with a kind of confession; a continuous confession is being made on stage in dialogue form; it was an exact replica of reality. Now this plan of the play got reduced more and more to words, because that means no objects on the stage, no problems on the stage. . . . So it was a process of reduction that was not intended but that simply happened.

Not surprisingly, then, *Self-Accusation* has many points of similarity to *Offending the Audience*. It too consists of a number of simple self-contained statements grouped into forty-one paragraphs of varying lengths without stage directions or assigned speeches, simply the opening instruction:

This piece is a *Sprechstück* for a male and a female speaker. There are no roles. The speakers, whose voices are synchronized with each other, speak alternately or in unison, softly or loudly, with very harsh transitions, so that an acoustic pattern emerges. The stage is bare. Both speakers work with microphones and loudspeakers. Auditorium and stage remain lighted throughout. The curtain is not used. Even at the end of the piece no curtain falls.

Again, as in *Offending the Audience*, there is an indication of a cyclic progression, with ideas introduced near the beginning of the piece picked up and qualified or redefined later on; and a director would have to try to discern sequences in the anonymous-looking paragraphs.

The piece falls into three sections of two to three pages each, followed by a final section of some thirteen pages. The first section, consisting of the first thirteen paragraphs, begins with the statement: "I came into the world." We are thus introduced at once to the central and only character of the piece, "I," as "I" tells how "I" was born and then proceeds to recount (though not quite in chronological order) the various natural stages of growth to full possession, awareness, and enjoyment of the most important of the faculties of mind and body. It is a sort of abstract autobiography: "I" is not a character or person in the conventional sense at all, a fact underlined by the speeches being shared by two people,

not even of the same sex. "I" is the word by which everyone refers to themselves, so the "I" of this piece is simply everyone, which explains why the many and various
actions recounted later on cannot have been performed
by one consistent individual. They are a mosaic of everyone's experience.

By the end of this first section, "I" can move, speak,
hear, see, name himself and the world around him using
grammatically correct sentences, and is aware of his own
capabilities and of the concepts of time, will, and responsibility. And with the realization that such potential
for unrestricted action as "I" now possesses must involve
the idea of responsibility, there comes a sudden shift of
gear into a second section, marked by following the
triumphant "I became a rational being" with a strong
qualification: "It was no longer just nature that I had to
obey. I had to obey rules." In other words, society will
not tolerate the unconditional exercise of an individual's
faculties. It imposes rules and restrictions within which
this exercise is permitted, and the moment someone becomes a full-fledged individual, he is subject to these
rules.

The second section (the fourteenth to the twenty-
first paragraph) is concerned with outlining the multi-
farious regulations, obligations, and liabilities that "I"
now has to take into account. This is epitomized in a
paragraph where each mental or physical faculty is set
against restrictions in its use: "I became capable of dis-
tinguishing between good and evil: I became obliged to
avoid evil. I became capable of playing by the rules of
the game: I became obliged to avoid infringing the rules
of the game." The section ends with an amusing parody
of a litany in which "I" asks which of a whole host of
varyingly vital and petty rules he has "sinned" against.

The final rhetorical question, "Have I sinned against the rules, plans, ideas, postulates, principles, etiquettes, statutes, public opinions, and formulae of the whole world?" is an expression of the total guilt induced in "I" by the myriad restraints imposed upon him.

If in the first section the development of "I" was positive and progressive (propounding a thesis) and in the second section it was negative and inhibited (propounding an antithesis), in the third section "I" can be said to make further advances, to gain more territory, but it is territory gained in knowledge of and in defiance of restrictive pressures (being a synthesis of the first two sections). For the third section (the twenty-second to the twenty-eighth paragraphs) and, indeed, the fourth section (the rest of the piece), which really forms a lengthy corollary to the third, are concerned with the need for "I" to express himself. Self-expression is the consummate affirmation of individuality, and the limitations that society places on self-expression reveal its desire to curb that individuality. "I," being semantically the epitome of individuality, explains how he went ahead and expressed himself in all manner of ways in defiance of society's explicit and implicit laws and taboos. To begin with, in the third section, these acts of self-expression are unmistakably antisocial: they include spitting, mistimed and misplaced demonstrations of approval, and litter-bugging. But the twenty-ninth paragraph, which commences the fourth section, lists a number of self-expressive activities whose normality and harmlessness seem unimpeachable: speaking, acquiring objects, procreating, manufacturing objects, looking, playing, walking. Most of these, however, are taken up again in subsequent paragraphs where, by the addition of ever more specific circumstances, the cumulative ef-

fect is to show that the original action has led more
often to a breach of regulations than not. Thus, although "looking" in itself is innocent enough, it is
shown to have led to looking at "objects that it was
shameless to look at," to not looking away from "events
that it was treasonable to watch," to not looking at
"people who spoke to me," to watching "films that were
not recommended," to watching "games without tickets," and to keeping "my eyes open during sexual inter-
course." This pattern of progression from general harmlessness to particular infringements, culminating in an
especially ludicrous instance of violation or of failure to
behave *comme il faut,* is used to demonstrate the impossibility of law-abiding self-expression through walking
(and moving), speaking, acquiring objects, looking (and
listening), ingesting (of air, food, drink, etc.), and playing. It will be noticed that many of these are precisely
the faculties whose acquisition and potential was so
triumphantly proclaimed at the beginning of the piece.
Now, toward the end, it is seen that the use of these
faculties to express the individual personality of their
owner is doomed to clash with the strictures of society.

The climax of the piece comes with the longest
paragraph almost at the end. The first sentences have a
mock-biblical ring to them, entirely appropriate to the
huge miscellany of "confessions" that follow. Each of
the "crimes against society" that are solemnly confessed
is a feature of individual personality or conscience rather
than an actual crime. But the main device is to make the
list so long and the majority of the "crimes" so petty and
ludicrous that the confession loses its validity and becomes instead a proud assertion of individuality, and the
final crescendo of irresponsible behavior in emergency
conditions becomes an almost existential act of defiance

in a chaotic world. Moreover, the last action, "I moved," while foolish and possibly fatal in this context, exactly and ironically echoes "I's" very first achievement after having been born: "I moved." Now all the achievements of the beginning of the play have been nullified or heavily qualified; all except one—the act of becoming. But this too is not allowed to stand; the penultimate sentences of the piece read: "I did not become what I ought to have become. I did not keep the promise that I could have kept." The original sin referred to so often in the piece is hardly the Christian doctrine; it is rather the original sin borne by every individual in his preordained inability to live within the dictates of society. Even the act of becoming is hedged around with social expectation.

The individual versus society—it is an old, old theme. But what Handke has done is to render it abstract and universal. Having as it were publicly forsworn fiction and illusionism in *Offending the Audience,* he now tackles a big theme without resorting to these devices, which have been the mainstay of playwrights before him, even of the antiillusionist Brecht and the antitheatrical Ionesco. Compare, for instance, *The Measures Taken (Die Maßnahme)* with *Self-Accusation.* Both are examinations of the individual's situation in the wider context of the community, but despite its theatrical unconventionality Brecht's play still makes its point by means of a fable in which fictional characters are impersonated by the performers. And while it is true that Esslin might be referring to Handke when he writes of Ionesco's attitude in *The Bald Prima Donna,* "What he deplores is the leveling of individuality, the acceptance of slogans by the masses, of ready-made ideas, which increasingly turn our mass societies into

collections of centrally directed automata," the difference is again one of method: Ionesco had to incarnate
the Smiths and the Martins as ultratypical products of
the mass society in order to dramatize his theme.
Handke has abstracted the same theme and at the same
time universalized it by making the central "character"
a blank first-person singular with an impossibly compre-
hensive case history so that every member of the audience can identify philosophically though not emotionally and fit his or her own features into the blank. "I" is
a sort of modern Everyman, except that Everyman for
all his archetypicality becomes very real to the audience
through his being physically impersonated and their
identifying emotionally with him, whereas "I" remains
an abstract concept, given voice but no substance. It is
the skill and thoroughness with which Handke has carried this idea through that gives the rather unprepos-
sessing texture of *Self-Accusation* its excitement and
interest.

4

ooooooooooooooooooooooooooooooooooooooooooo

Cries

for Help

H andke's fourth and last *Sprechstück, Cries for Help,* either works completely or not at all. And its success depends so much on qualities in performance that it is not possible here to do more than discuss its intentions. For *Cries for Help* is like a revue sketch, both in its length (four and a half pages, or about ten minutes) and in its use of a single situation on which to hang a climactic punch line. The idea is best expressed in Handke's own introduction to the piece:

as many people as one likes can work together on this *sprechstück*: at least two are needed, however (who can be male or female). the speakers' task is to show the way over many sentences and words to the word they are seeking, HELP. the need for help is performed acoustically to the audience, divorced from an actual, particular situation. the sentences and words are moreover spoken not in their usual sense but in the sense of seeking for help. . . . on the way to the word help, the speakers again and again get into proximity with the word they are seeking, in terms of sense or even only in terms of sound: depending on this proximity, the respective reply of NO, which follows each attempt, also alters.

It all sounds very much like the children's game, Hunt the Thimble, where the clues the onlookers may give to the seeker are restricted verbally to degrees of temperature, but where much more information is in fact conveyed by the varying volume, urgency, and number of the onlookers' voices. Handke's own analogy is his favorite one of the football match, where the intensity of the spectators' shouts varies according to how near the ball is to the goal.

As usual, the piece is made up of a number of paragraphs, each of which consists of a series of miscellaneous statements, all but one of which are followed by the reply: NO. The one exception is of course the final successful guess: "help?" About halfway through, the statements cease to be full sentences and become short phrases and eventually single words. This could hardly fail to produce an accelerating tempo, whose compulsiveness must play a considerable part in the resolution of the whole piece. Here Handke is verging again, as he did in his "Rules for the Actors" preceding *Offending the Audience*, on territory first mapped out by Artaud, who insisted that the sound of words in the theater could be and should be more evocative and meaningful than their sense. These are concepts whose truth can only be tested in the theater, and critical analysis from the page can go no further in this direction.

That Handke believes in their truth is evident from his assertion in his introduction that the audience will quickly realize the word that is being sought and might indeed call it out, like children at a Punch and Judy show warning the other puppets of the approach of the crocodile. This seems to be wishful thinking; it is unlikely that an uninitiated audience would understand what was going on sufficiently well to respond in this way, although they might be prompted by the fact that many of the statements relate to situations in which help might really be required. The statements themselves appear to be culled from public announcements ("unemployment has dropped further"), newspaper reports ("the actor suffered an attack of faintness while actually on stage"), notices and instructions ("breakfast included in the price," "tear here"), spoken and written officialese ("fill in carefully in block letters"), domestic and moral maxims ("a cripple cannot help being a cripple"), slogans ("no more war"), and words of command and exclamation ("hands up!" "bravo!"). They represent Handke's most blatant use to date of verbal "ready-mades." In his earlier pieces, he had already shown a tendency toward words and phrases that had sunk to the level of platitude or banality through over-use in everyday speech. This could be seen as a product of his wish to avoid personal lyricism. Now, however, he has gone a step further, confining himself exclusively to extracts from the language of newspapers, slot machines, medicine bottles, road signs, and so on. As with Marcel Duchamp's three-dimensional "ready-mades," as with the collages from magazines and advertisements by pop artists like Richard Hamilton, or even as with certain concrete poets who play with the patterns made by an ordinary word or phrase, the artistic act is no longer one of creation from virgin material but of selection of al-ready available material and its placing in a context.

Handke's selection for his verbal pop-collage is often entertaining and witty, particularly in the juxta-position of certain phrases. It is interesting too that the "ready-made" poems that appear in *The Inner World of the Outer World of the Inner World* date from soon after the first performance of *Cries for Help*. How does this collage technique relate to the intention of the piece? Handke explains the intention in the introduc-tion:

While the speakers are seeking the *word* help, they need *help*; but then, when they have finally found the *word* help, they have no more need of *help* . . . they are re-lieved that they can call for help. The word HELP has lost its meaning.

One interpretation of this paradox is that the débris of slogans and platitudes, which is all that society bequeaths the individual by way of means of expression, is sadly inadequate for the expression of something genuine like a call for help. This is a well-worn theme, particularly beloved of the absurdists and of off-off-Broadway playwrights such as Jean-Claude van Itallie, whose plays are full of human cries of anguish drowned in the hubbub and indifference of the modern city.

But Handke also states that a word, in this case the word for help, can lose its meaning because its meaning has already been sufficiently communicated by the "ready-made" phrases preceding it, which normally have no ability to communicate such a meaning. Even the most familiar phrases, then, can be made to change their meaning according to circumstance. In earlier pieces Handke seemed concerned to strip language (as well as theater) to its bare essentials. Now even those bare essentials are questioned: words have no absolute meaning; their meaning can be made to vary. This concept, again, is not new, although it is more likely to be encountered in a philosophical treatise than on stage. It is presented confusedly in *Cries for Help* and is likely to be missed by an uninitiated audience. It forms the basis, however, of Handke's next play, *Kaspar*, which deals with the question of how language can be made to change and lose its meaning. In this light, *Cries for Help* can be seen as an interesting experiment, which marks the transition from Handke's *Sprechstücke* to his first major play.

5

∘∘∘

Kaspar

Even the title of Handke's first full-length play signals a new development. Kaspar is after all a name, the name of the central figure, and no figure with a name has hitherto appeared in Handke's plays. More than this, Kaspar represents an actual historical personage, Kaspar Hauser, who mysteriously turned up from nowhere in Nuremberg in 1828, aged sixteen, but with the mind of a child. Ernst Jandl's short poem "16 years," chosen by Handke to preface his play, can be seen as referring obliquely to Hauser and his limited powers of speech, as it asks lispingly: "what thall/he do/the lad/with hith/thickthteen yearth." But, hardly surprisingly, *Kaspar* is not a dramatized historical biography. "The play *Kaspar* does not show how THINGS REALLY ARE or REALLY WERE with Kaspar Hauser," reads the first line of Handke's introduction. "It shows what is POSSIBLE with someone. It shows how someone can be brought to speech by speech. The play could also be called *Speech-Torture* [*Sprechfolterung*]." In fact, the play was originally provisionally entitled *Speech* (*Sprechen*), which makes the link with the *Sprechstücke* even stronger.

It is, of course, the metaphorical implications of Hauser's predicament, rather than the historical details, which have attracted Handke as they have attracted many writers before him: the implications of a near-adult apparently coming into contact with the world for the first time, a human being with the physical and mental potential of a man, but with that potential quite undeveloped—the implications in fact of being born a fully grown man. As Handke explained to Artur Joseph:

In *Kaspar Hauser* I discovered the prototype of a kind of linguistic myth. The figure made me curious. A human being who for sixteen or seventeen years has lived in a

58

wooden compartment suddenly comes into the outside world and has to make himself familiar with it, although he cannot speak. . . . This Kaspar Hauser appeared interesting to me not merely as a mythical figure, but as a prototype of people who do not get on with themselves and the world around them, who feel themselves isolated.

This myth is presented on stage by means of an abstraction of the central situation from the concrete historical circumstances. Kaspar thus becomes a timeless, backgroundless Everyman figure, much as the "I" in *Self-Accusation* was an abstraction of everyone. Indeed the themes and development of the two plays are markedly similar, with one significant difference: in the earlier piece the gradual growth by "I" to full mental and physical power and the cumulative restrictions placed on him are recounted *in the past tense*; in *Kaspar*, because of the central hypothesis that Kaspar is a newborn adult, the audience can be *shown* his subsequent development as it takes place, which makes for infinitely more theatrical impact.

If Kaspar bears only an abstract relationship to his historical namesake, he might be expected to be more concretely related to his theatrical namesake, the Kaspar of the Punch and Judy show. Indeed there is much of the puppet about Kaspar. His first blundering entrance, his unsteady gait, his tendency to walk into things, his set expression (Handke directs that the actor wear a mask—a mask depicting perpetual astonishment), all are reminiscent of a string puppet, and the actor might well adopt this as his "style" for the part.

But another aspect of the puppet, its manipulability, is more sinisterly relevant. The play shows Kaspar brought to a state in which he is unable to initiate speech or action of his own free will. If at the beginning of the play he looks like a puppet, by the end of the play he has become one, though he no longer looks like one. This sinister aspect is emphasized by Handke's saying that Kaspar resembles Frankenstein's monster or King Kong, the one a creature made of human parts and artificially imbued with life, which runs amok destroying itself and its creator, the other a giant gorilla brought by man from its natural habitat to the city, where it also runs amok destroying half of New York. Kaspar's life, too, is crucially dictated by man-made forces outside himself; true, he does not run amok, but there is an inference that Handke is suggesting this (at least to his audience) as an untried alternative to submission.

Handke also states that "Kaspar has no similarity to a clown [*Spaßmacher*]," which he seems to deny in the description of Kaspar's get-up. It is certainly not the costume of a traditional clown: not grotesque enough for the Auguste's, except for his baggy trousers, and not elegant enough for the white-faced Joey's, despite Kaspar's pallid mask. (In the circus world the red-faced, baggy-trousered clown is known as an Auguste, while the white-faced, pantalooned clown who derives from the pierrot and the harlequin is called a Joey.) It seems rather (and this is the intention) to have been assembled at random from a theatrical wardrobe. But this, after all, was how Chaplin made up his legendary outfit. If, in appearance, Kaspar is something of a cross between a clown and a knockabout comic, then the antics he is made to perform heighten this impression. His fumbling effort to find the gap in the curtains through which to enter is a standard music-hall routine, as is the bit where he puts his hand into a crevice in the sofa, gets it stuck, puts in his other hand to help, and gets that stuck, too. And just to confuse the issue further, a critic who saw Peymann's production of the play at Frankfurt described Kaspar's first appearance as that of an "Arlecchino" and a *"commedia dell'arte* figure." What all these figures have in common is their theatricality (they do not exist per se in real life) and their popular appeal (or else they would not have survived). Both these factors work in Handke's favor: the theatricalization is part of his abstraction and generalization of the figure, while remaining within the confines of the "pure play," which must exist on the same plane of reality as the audience; and the popularity of the figure, showing as it does much of the appeal of the "underdog" or "little man," aids its acceptance as Everyman. Handke's denial of the figure's clownishness presumably stems from a Brechtian fear that recognition of a funny and lovable stereotype (rather than a sinister monster) will prevent the audience from seeing the serious implications of Kaspar's fate and its application to their own society. This problem can only be solved in production by trying to strike the right balance between the sympathetic figure at the beginning and the horror of what he becomes; and indeed there have been as many different Kaspars as there have been productions of the play, many of them going for a maskless, more or less ordinary-looking figure.

The play itself is, like the *Sprechstücke,* divided into paragraphs, but there the resemblance ends. For the paragraphs (numbered 1 to 65) disguise a much more conventional structure. For instance, much of the play consists of extremely detailed stage directions, leaving much less to the director and actors than did the previous pieces. (His next play, incidentally, consists of nothing but stage directions.) There is also apportionment of dialogue between Kaspar and the *Einsager* (a made-up word meaning "in-sayers" but having something of the force of "indoctrinators" or "persuaders"), whose job it is to "bring Kaspar to speech by speech." In *Kaspar* the two sets of speeches are printed side by side on a vertically divided page, which serves to indicate exactly how the dialogue should overlap. Furthermore, the play is punctuated by a number of blackouts, which have the effect of dividing the play into short scenes, and it is these, rather than the imperceptible paragraphs, that the audience would take to be the stages by which the play progresses.

The action of the first scene up to the first blackout (paragraphs 1–15) is closest to the historical incidents that gave Handke the idea for the play. Kaspar "can hardly walk," Handke explained to Artur Joseph:

He has been lying down for practically seventeen years. That is not discernible from history. I took this situation over and decked it out with historical quotations from Kaspar Hauser's autobiography. He describes there what he felt like on the first evening, after he came out into the world. He had only one sentence at his disposal: "I would like to become a horseman such as my father once was" ("A söchener Reiter möcht i wärn, wie mei Voter aner gween is"). He wakes up suddenly in the middle of the night in a strange room and feels pain because he had never walked before. He sees a green stove in the room, and it glows in the night. And Kaspar wants to unbosom himself to it and goes to it and says to it the only sentence at his disposal: "I would like to become a horseman such as my father once was." He doesn't know that things cannot hear or answer him, but he says the sentence when he is hungry, or when he is getting on well. He cannot express himself in any other way.

Handke has theatricalized this course of events by transforming the room into a stage haphazardly set with an assortment of props and stage furniture, by transmuting Hauser's awakening into Kaspar's stumbling and astonished eruption onto the stage, and by abstracting his only sentence into: "I would like to become such as someone else once was" ("Ich möcht ein solcher werden wie einmal ein andrer gewesen ist"). As Kaspar blunders around the stage, upsetting the furniture and repeating his sentence, he kicks open the wardrobe doors, and at this moment the *Einsager,* three or more disembodied, dispassionate voices, are heard over the loudspeakers, commending the multiple uses to which Kaspar can put his sentence. Their conclusion—that "with the sentence you learn there is order, and with the sentence you learn to learn order"—is ironically contrasted with the image of Kaspar, now silent and still amid the chaos he has created.

The *Einsager's* next step is to destroy Kaspar's one precious sentence, the only intellectual concept that he brought with him into the world. In Handke's words: "Through their speech they eradicate this sentence from him. . . . That is the first phase. The *Einsager* have brought him to dumbness." Now they indoctrinate him, painfully and confusingly, in conventional speech and in the conventional precepts of good order and moral conformity. Thus bombarded, Kaspar sets himself and the stage to rights, his actions according more and more with the *Einsager's* rhythmic recitation of moral maxims.

There follows a sort of baptism by darkness, by which the *Einsager* demonstrate to Kaspar that his new command of speech can be used to overcome such elemental (and unsocial) emotions as fear of the dark; after which Kaspar is taught a variety of grammatical constructions. His first attempts at imitation are interesting surreal distortions, but gradually he produces the required stereotypes. His final, triumphant use of the verb "to be"—"I am who I am," with its divine and existential echoes—is followed, however, by a glimpse of the allegedly conquered darkness beneath the brilliant surface: "Why are there nothing but black serpents flying about?" (a quotation, by way of homage, from the recently rediscovered Austro-Hungarian playwright, Ödön von Horvàth).

Seventeen short scenes follow (paragraphs 32–57), in which a number of identical, masked Kaspar figures perform little sketches to demonstrate, for Kaspar's benefit, such elementary phenomena as movement, pain, noise, sound. Now fully aware of the world around him, Kaspar, alone on stage, successfully shuts the wardrobe door and delivers an elegant manifesto of his new persona. He is the apotheosis of orderliness. He even begins to speak in rhymed verse. "The world is actually rhymed for him," says Handke. "Now," affirms Kaspar, "I would no longer like to be someone else." He leaves the stage; but, sinisterly, the wardrobe doors swing open again. Blackout. Interval.

Much as Handke suggests that before the play begins his opening stage directions be repeated softly over loudspeakers as the audience enters the auditorium, so for the interval he suggests a sound collage to be beamed at the audience in the foyer, the bars, and even in the street outside the theater! The text he provides seems to allude mainly to violent political action, but near the end it changes to a lucid account of dinner-table etiquette. But the instructions are increasingly interspersed with "rogue" sentences (like subliminal inserts in a film, or the one thing "wrong" in a Magritte) that are full of actual or implied violence. "The soup is served from the right. . . . The stranglehold comes from both sides." It seems to be the very orderliness of the domestic scene (directly related to Kaspar's newly ordered life) that has occasioned the violence by repressing all "undesirable" expressions of emotion. It is this thread that runs throughout the second half of the play.

The first scene (paragraphs 60–64) begins with the *Einsager* reciting a paean (in the same irregularly rhymed verse used earlier by Kaspar) in praise of beating people up to bring them to order. Meanwhile, five of the duplicate Kaspars, their masks (and Kaspar's) now expressing contentment, not astonishment, seat themselves on the sofa ready to provide a cacophonous accompaniment to Kaspar's speech to the audience listing the restrictions that society imposes on its members and the code of behavior it exacts from them. With this speech (amplified through the *Einsager*'s loudspeakers) Kaspar turns on the audience, as the *Einsager* had turned on him. But just as his earlier integration was undermined by glimpses of the abyss beneath, so here his confident bullying ends in the thrice repeated "Jeder Satz ist für die Katz" (approximately: "All words are for the birds")—a negation of all that the *Einsager* have taught him.

The complex speeches that follow reveal chiefly the disturbingly arbitrary connection between a phenomenon and the word used to describe it; thus, Kaspar recalls, when he learned the word "snow," he applied it to everything white and then to anything at all, with the result that both the word and snow itself ceased to have any meaning for him. As Handke told Artur Joseph, the play examines "the impossibility of *expressing* something with language: that is, to say something that goes beyond the actual sentence into the significant and the meaningful."

A further crescendo of nerve-jangling noise, with the Kaspars advancing toward the audience, climaxes in Kaspar's cry: "I am brought to speech. I am transferred into reality." But he is answered with silence and darkness.

When the lights come on again for the short final scene, Kaspar continues speaking, but his words just fail to make sense. At the same time, the other Kaspars busy themselves ridiculing "an object, perhaps a chair," rendering it "IMPOSSIBLE" by depriving it of its meaning as a chair; and the *Einsager* are endlessly repeating: "May be," referring partly to the fluidity of meaning revealed by all the Kaspars, and partly to Kaspar's final words: "I am I only by chance," a pathetic distortion of his earlier triumphant "I am who I am." Kaspar has now realized that, since the *Einsager* (representing environmental and societal pressures) have had so much control over his development, he cannot claim to be an absolute product of his own individual qualities; and, more fundamentally, he has realized that since the meaning of language, the medium through which he has developed perception and personality, is arbitrary and relative and can be altered by forces outside himself, he too can claim only an arbitrary and contingent egoity. He can define himself only in relation to shifting standards. With this devastating realization, the curtain jerks closed, knocking over all the Kaspars like tailor's dummies. The play is over.

In the course of the play Handke has invented some neat devices to illustrate his abstract theme. Some of these, such as the use of rhyme to indicate the acme of Kaspar's powers of speech and social integration, can be fully appreciated from the text alone; others, such as the use of multiple Kaspars to demonstrate different areas of perception, are more effective in the theater, although it is never clear whether they are meant to be the original Kaspar split into several bodies for purposes of theatrical demonstration, or whether they are the mass-produced human beings of a society that molds every human being into an identical form. But there are also echoes of other men's plays and of other men's philosophies.

The play that is perhaps most like *Kaspar* is Beckett's *Act without Words I*, which Handke saw performed at the same Experimenta that launched his own *Offending the Audience* in 1966. *Act without Words I* shares with *Kaspar* a central, abstract, generalized, Everyman figure (the sole figure on stage in Beckett's play is called "the man") whose behavior is ruthlessly shaped by unseen but audible forces offstage, an amount of almost knock-about physical action and, the educative process completed, a desolate ending. Beckett, too, has theatricalized a situation that might well have been presented in more concrete, naturalistic terms. Thus "the man" is repeatedly summoned into the wings by whistles only to be flung back on stage every time, until he no longer responds to the whistles. Beckett is less interested than Handke in the nature of the offstage forces, but in both plays Pavlovian methods of instruction are used. And Kaspar, too, starts by suffering from the Cartesian gap between mind and body, between situation and action, which is the bane of so many of Beckett's "clowns" (Beckett also uses a shorthand of recognizable theatrical stereotypes). "The time lapse between the decision and the action is a reminder that the connection between the two is not necessarily a simple one," as one Beckett critic put it. That Kaspar appears to close this gap, to become integrated, is merely a veneer that society demands that its members acquire. It is true that Beckett's concern is less with the individual *vis-à-vis* society than with the individual faced with the void that is life, but his presentation of a theatricalized typical individual has considerable bearing on Handke's solution of a similar problem in *Kaspar*.

The dramatization of the conflict between society and the individual in which the one attempts to mold the other is not new, even to Handke, who had tackled this theme in *Self-Accusation*. There would be little point in cataloguing all previous treatments of this conflict in the theater, but two deserve particular mention. One is the Living Theater's *Frankenstein*, whose monster Handke had said Kaspar resembles. Jeremy Kingston described the performance in *Punch*:

The company are shot, beheaded, gassed, racked, hung, or otherwise executed all over the huge three-tier scaffolding that forms the bulk of the acting area. Dr. Frankenstein . . . then begins the reconstruction of a new creature. Indoctrination follows, with all the woes attendant on an industrial civilization, and in the last act the cells in the scaffolding fill with prisoners of the state, each going individually mad.

The parallel to *Kaspar* is close, especially as both plays start with the inhuman process of wiping the slate clean, by mass murder in *Frankenstein* or by obliterating Kaspar's only sentence.

The second interesting treatment of "the individual cowed into conformism by society and convention" is, inevitably, Ionesco's, and these words are used by Martin Esslin to describe the theme of both *Jacques or Obedience* and *The Lesson*. In *Jacques*, conformist society is represented by calling all the members of one family

Jacques, just as "three-quarters of the inhabitants of the town" in *The Bald Prima Donna* are called Bobby Watson, which relates to Handke's device of multiple Kaspars (Ionesco even states that "all the characters, except Jacques, can wear masks"). More significantly, the metaphor of domination in both Ionesco plays is *language*: Jacques at first refuses to pronounce the words that would confirm his acceptance of his family's standards, but, after exclaiming "Words! What crimes are committed in your name," he accepts the bourgeois creed "I love potatoes in their jackets!" as his own; and *The Lesson* has become one of the classic theatrical demonstrations of the use of language as an instrument of power. In a sense, *Kaspar* combines features from both plays in that the *Einsager* use language as in *The Lesson* to bring an individual into line with conformist standards as in *Jacques*.

Still more interesting is Ionesco's explanation in *Notes and Counter-Notes* of what happened to the ending of *The Bald Prima Donna*:

Unfortunately the wise and elementary truths [the Smiths and Martins] exchanged, when strung together, had gone mad, the language had become disjointed, the characters distorted. . . . For me, what had happened was a kind of collapse of reality. The words had turned into sounding shells devoid of meaning; . . . the world appeared to me in an unearthly, perhaps its true, light, beyond understanding and governed by arbitrary laws.

This applies almost word for word to *Kaspar*, and it is closely matched by what Handke says about that play's ending:

And then [Kaspar] acts as if broken, then falls more and

more into confusion, then his speech suddenly begins to go wrong—until complete schizophrenia sets in, complete tohubohu, an upside down world governs the stage; in the end, chaos.

Ionesco offers a note of interpretation:

The text of *The Bald Prima Donna* . . . consisting as it did of ready-made expressions and the most threadbare clichés, revealed to me all that is automatic in the language and behavior of people: "talking for the sake of talking," talking because there is nothing personal to say, the absence of any life within, the mechanical routine of every-day life, man sunk in his social background, no longer able to distinguish himself from it.

Kaspar breaks down because the language he has been taught is similarly automatic and tailored to the norms of society.

Philosophically the basis of *Kaspar* is that, as language is necessary for the expression of thought (and may even be a prerequisite for thought itself), he who is in a position to control people's language also controls their thought. The *Einsager* are in just such a position *vis-à-vis* Kaspar. Kaspar comes into the world possessing one sentence. This sentence is all he has but it is uniquely his. But because it fails to impose order on the world around him, and because it is his sentence and not theirs, the *Einsager* systematically destroy it and replace it with a language whose expressive power is limited to the reiteration of social conformism. This means that even if Kaspar were to think nonconformist or just individual thoughts, he would have no language to express them.

This is like a parody of Wittgenstein's thesis in *Tractatus logico-philosophicus*, in the Preface to which the author writes:

The aim of the book is to set a limit to thought, or rather—not to thought, but to the expression of thoughts. . . . It will therefore only be in language that the limit can be set, and what lies on the other side of the limit will simply be nonsense.

Handke endorses this view in *Kaspar*, but the benevolent philosopher attempting to define the limits of language and, therefore, of the expression of thought is replaced by the tyrannic *Einsager*. This is not to say that Handke is deriding Wittgenstein. On the contrary, much of Handke's writing is a literary counterpart to Wittgenstein's logical positivism in its rejection of the metaphysical and its acceptance only of that reality that can be verified by the physical senses. Ever since his first reading from *The Peddler* at Gruppe 47, critics have been remarking on the similarity of Handke's style to Wittgenstein's in its tendency to approach a phenomenon over and over again from different angles in an attempt to define its absolute reality.

In *Kaspar* Handke is accepting Wittgenstein's view of the limitability of language but is illustrating what happens when the limits are set by the "wrong" people. Who actually are the *Einsager*? Handke refuses to say: "No concrete social system is being criticized in *Kaspar*, neither the capitalist nor the socialist system." The *Einsager* then are intended to be an abstract representation of any force that attempts control of language and, therefore, of thought. But the language they themselves use is too steeped in bourgeois values to remain entirely abstract.

And when Handke offers a political interpretation of *Kaspar*, it is clearly prejudiced in favor of the Left:

What upsets me is people's estrangement from their own language. . . . People who are estranged from their language and their speech are like the workers estranged from their products, who are also estranged from the world.

The second part of Wittgenstein's statement is also illustrated in the play: "what lies on the other side of the limit will simply be nonsense." When Kaspar realizes that the language he has been taught is so limited as to be virtually useless ("Jeder Satz ist für die Katz"), he gradually slips into nonsense as he tries to transcend those limits and achieve meaningful self-expression.

Kaspar, then, has several levels of meaning. It could be taken simply as a theatricalization of Everyman's life cycle: birth (onto the stage); growth of awareness and physical integration; acquisition of speech; responsibility for one's own and others' behavior; finally, decay of one's mental faculties; and death (as the curtain closes). Seen as social comment, the play is an abstract demonstration of the way an individual's individuality is stirpped from him by society, specifically by limiting the expressive power of the language it teaches him. "This neutering of language, at once repressive and cunning, is one dominant tendency of its adversary, language control" (Günter Eich). Politically, this criticism can be applied to any person or group in power, but it is phrased in such a way that middle-of-the-road or right-wing governments seem most impeached. Philosophically, *Kaspar* is a dramatization of the connection between language and thought and an examination of the limits that can be set on both. Handke's achievement is to have invented a dramatic form that succeeds for a large part of the time in conveying all these levels of meaning at once.

6

ooooooooooooooooooooooooooooooooooooooooo

My Foot
My Tutor

"What we cannot speak about we must consign to silence" was how Wittgenstein concluded his *Tractatus logico-philosophicus*. And this statement forms both the implicit conclusion of *Kaspar* and the implicit premise of Handke's next play, *My Foot My Tutor*. Kaspar, at the end of the play, had discovered that the language that had been taught him was useless. It could not express what he wanted to say. *My Foot My Tutor* leads on from this: it is an hour-long play in which not a word is spoken. But again it is a play concerned with presenting an aspect of the learning process, of the way in which an individual becomes aware that he has to conform to forces outside himself that wish to mold him in their likeness. In *Self-Accusation* these forces were referred to obliquely in the past; in *Kaspar* they made themselves audible as the *Einsager*; now, in *My Foot My Tutor* they are incarnated in the single figure of the "guardian" exerting his silent sway over the "ward" ("What! The ward wants to be guardian?" being the German version of Prospero's line, "What, I say, My foot my tutor!" which is the epigraph to Handke's play). The crucial relationship between these two men is illustrated in ten short scenes, punctuated as in *Kaspar* by blackouts and consisting of simple actions presented without recourse to speech.

In *Kaspar*, Handke had forsaken antiillusionism so far as to put on stage a figure in costume, albeit a figure whose theatricality was evident. In *My Foot My Tutor*, the two figures wear the realistic costumes of farm workers—blue bib overalls, vest, and heavy shoes for the young ward, and for the older guardian gray working trousers, muddy Wellington boots, and an open-necked shirt with the sleeves rolled up to reveal tattooed arms —and they act in realistic sets outside and inside a farmhouse. The realism is, however, firmly theatricalized by giving both figures half-masks and by demanding that the painted vista of cornfields and turnip fields shall look like what it is—a painted vista—an effect admirably achieved in Claus Peymann's production of the première, by resorting to the preposterous trompe l'oeil technique of the nineteenth-century theater, a technique whose outdatedness renders it theatrical in the extreme. As hitherto with Handke, then, the events onstage can be said to have no aspirations to any reality beyond their theatrical reality. Technically, we are still in the world of the "pure play."

The play opens with the ward (Handke refers to him throughout as "das Mündel") sitting on a stool outside the farmhouse eating first one apple, then another. "For a moment," wrote an English critic at a performance in Belgrade, "it seemed the author was engaging on stimulating the audience into some aggressive reaction against the fact that nothing whatsoever was going on." But Handke's intention is that the scene shall radiate a "deep tranquility," a sense even of innocent contentment due to be broken up by the entrance of the guardian, who simply stands and stares at the ward until the ward is stared into stopping eating. As he does so the lights slowly fade. In mood and shape this scene parallels the beginning of *Self-Accusation* with its report of triumphant progress until the mention of rules alters the speakers' tone, and of *Kaspar* with its sense of innocent exploration until the *Einsager* break into the proceedings. In all three cases there is a sense of an uncontaminated, unrestricted innocence coming up against a dominating force. In the darkness following this scene, Handke prescribes the amplified sound of breathing that he has seen used as an intimidation tactic in an Italian

B film and with which he now intends to frighten his
audience—partly for the sake of it, and partly presumably to underline the menace inherent in the relationship between the two men. Conveniently, it also gives
time to change the set to the interior of the farmhouse,
doll's-houselike in its simplicity, with one door, one
window, one table, and two chairs.

As the lights had faded out on the previous scene,
music had been faded in. The music, specified as an
instrumental by Country Joe and the Fish (Handke is
still a connoisseur of rock), is to be heard throughout
the rest of the play. The second scene consists of three
simple "lessons," in each of which the guardian demonstrates his dominance and the ward learns subservience.
First, the guardian is reading a newspaper (which the
ward has fetched for him). Showing a childlike eager-
ness to imitate his elder, the ward begins reading a tiny
book. But, like a child, he seems to tire of this and begins drawing all over the book instead, and then all over
his hands and arms as if trying to give himself tattoos
like the guardian's. Meanwhile, the guardian has been
folding his paper over and over again until it is a crum-
pled mess in his fist. He stares at the ward until the
scribbling stops. In the second "lesson," the guardian
bends forward lower and lower in his chair; the ward
imitates him but is suitably always one stage lower than
the other man, ending in a sitting position with his head
between his knees and his knees closed over his head
("if possible," says the script). And the third "lesson"
is much the same but with greater visual impact, as the
guardian first gets as high up as he can and then as low
down as possible, while the ward, like a good adjutant,
maintains a position one degree lower in every case.

As the lights come up for the next scene the two

men are again sitting either side of the table. This is their position at the beginning of each of the interior scenes, and it begins to take on a formal, ritual quality like the ceremonial before a judo match. In this scene the guardian takes off his boots and his socks and begins cutting his toenails. The ward, acting the lackey as his master conducts his toilet, tidies away the boots, socks, and nail clippings. Then, as the guardian begins on his fingernails, the ward goes to a block calendar on the wall and tears off a page for every snip of the scissors—this cinematic cliché for time passing being used here, perhaps, to denote the endless monotony of the lackey's existence. Even so, the guardian gets the better of him: the calendar runs out of pages before the guardian finishes his nails. Again the ward is left inactive and immobile as the scene ends.

The fourth scene moves to another area of human activity—catering. With the aid of a hose attached to a tap offstage, the guardian fills a kettle and puts it on to boil. He then expertly winds the hose up. The ward is left with the unskilled labor of grinding the coffee, but when the kettle starts whistling, the ward gradually stops grinding.

The fifth scene is an interesting combination of school lesson and religious service, with the guardian simultaneously playing the parts of schoolmaster and priest, chalk in one hand and incense in the other. Correspondingly, the ward plays the part of the naughty schoolboy throwing burrs at the schoolmaster/priest when his back is turned. Again the ritual of domination is performed as the guardian, incense in hand, stares the ward into passivity.

The tiny sixth scene poses considerable problems for actor and stage manager alike. For a long time the two figures sit in their usual positions staring into space. Suddenly the ward's nose begins to bleed and goes on bleeding (the guardian takes no notice) as the lights fade.

The next scene shows Handke's erratic theatrical genius at its best and is the scene most commented on by critics who have attended stage performances of the play. What is so striking about one man first spinning another on the spot and then throwing a succession of bottles, plates, and glasses toward him, which he persistently, but uncomically, fails to catch? There is an element of audience assault about it, if only because the repeated noise of breaking glass and the willful wastage involved will get on most audiences' nerves when they are refused the outlet of laughter with which they are used to greeting such destructive goings-on in slapstick films. But more than this, the episode serves to depict a degree of cruelty in the guardian's treatment of the ward, which would be unbearable if it had not been transmuted into theatrical terms in this way. It is this element of cruelty, of the guardian's continued insistence that the ward catch the bottles, plates, and glasses when the guardian has deliberately made him too giddy to do anything at all, that gives the end of the scene its shock effect. Suddenly, as if quite by chance, the ward does in fact catch something. Suddenly, even if only accidentally, the ward has exercised a skill the guardian thought he did not possess. Suddenly the ward is on an equal footing with the guardian and to emphasize the shock, the play's only blackout occurs at this moment.

With the lights on again for the eighth scene, guardian and ward are again sitting at the table. The guardian gets up, but for the first time he is indecisive. As he walks around the room apparently wondering what to do, the ward gets up and follows him, copying his every move. In what might be seen as a final effort to demonstrate his superiority, the guardian dodges outside and slams the door after him before the ward can follow. The ward is nonplussed for a moment, then quickly crawls outside through a cat-flap in the door, which the audience "now see for the first time," says the script hopefully.

The scene is now changed back to the exterior set, and the proceedings recommence with the unveiling of a mysterious object that was intended to attract our curiosity in the first scene. It turns out to be a hand-operated machine for cutting the tops off turnips, and the following scene consists of the guardian showing the ward how to work the machine and the ward having indifferent success with it. This slightly sinister business is followed, when the lights go out, by a reprise of the sound of breathing, which gets gradually overwhelmingly loud until it suddenly cuts out.

After a long period of silence, the lights come up on a stage cleared of all props, furniture, and people but still showing the fields and the front of the farmhouse. The tenth and final scene gets under way as the ward comes on, having taken off his overalls, and performs a despairful variation on the earlier coffeemaking scene. This time the ward places the hose in a tin bathtub, turns the water on, and begins an apparently endless process of dropping sand handful by handful into the water in the bath. He is still doing this as the lights fade and the curtain comes down.

When faced with a play like this, it is difficult for a modern audience to resist the temptation to treat the action as metaphor, as material to be "interpreted." They can see what it *is*, but what does it *mean*? This

approach fails to take account of the fact that all the
scenes, when explained in words, must lose in multi-
plicity of association, even if they gain in specificity, because action is so much more richly ambiguous than
words. The ambiguity of the actions is further enhanced
by the actors' enforced lack of facial expression (they
wear masks) and by Handke's rigorous exclusion of any
display of mood or temperament on the part of the
characters. What we are left with is a sort of archetypal
dominant figure and an archetypal subservient figure
who perform a number of actions, some of which set
up associative reverberations, and who use a number of
objects, most of which can be taken as symbols of something else.

The first scene, for instance, where the guardian
inhibits the ward's peaceful apple eating, has a considerable power in its pure theatrical form: it is a sort of
distillation of intrusion, threat, and domination. But
does the apple, say, have any extra significance beyond
its apple-ness? Perhaps it represents food in general; and
the superior's evident disapproval of the inferior's activity represents the moral sanction of an employer over
an employee: namely, thou shalt not eat until thou hast
labored. Or, more generally, by eating the apple, sitting
in the sun, doing nothing, the inferior can forget his
inferior status until he is rudely reminded of it by the
arrival of his superior.

In the second scene, the three "lessons" again work
well on their own theatrical terms, particularly the continuous efforts of the inferior to imitate but to remain
one pace behind the superior: a distillation of servility.
But does the business with the newspaper and the little
book have some special meaning? The ward behaves
like a bored child having to do homework in the op-

pressive presence of a stern parent; the guardian is like
an impatient father disciplining his child. Can the
climbing up and down now be seen as a child's natural
attempt to find his own feet by imitating his parent and
that parent's repressive reaction to the possibility of being outstripped by his own child? And if the relationship in this scene is that of parent to child, in the third
scene it might be that of master to servant, in the fourth
scene chef to kitchen boy, in the fifth scene schoolmaster and priest to pupil and communicant, and so on.

It is possible to "interpret" the whole play along
these lines, prompted by such commonplace symbolism
as attaches to, say, incense, but every attempt to impose
one consistent system of metaphor on the relationship
of the two men goes against the effort Handke is making to abstract from this relationship its essential qualities—qualities that far exceed the specific functions suggested by specific labels; hence the abandonment of
words. Just as *Kaspar* presented an abstraction of the
actual problem that once faced the historical Kaspar
Hauser, so in *My Foot My Tutor* Handke has abstracted
the common factors in all relationships between a dominant and a subservient human being.

It is, however, important to mention, in parenthe-
sis, that Handke himself has hinted that the play is a
specific political parable. From the repeated use of the
word *Mitbestimmung* (codetermination) in a collage
designed by Handke and others to accompany an article
on the play in the March 1969 issue of *Theater Heute,*
it would appear that he wishes the play to be seen as a
theatricalization of shared problems on the labor and
student fronts, much as *Kaspar* was a theatricalization
of the pressures exerted by society on an individual.
"*Mitbestimmung*" is the current campaign cry of the

German Trade Unions Congress and demands that labor should have a voice in management. It also refers
by extension to the wish of students to participate in
the running of the universities. (And, more recently, to
the wish of actors to participate in the running of their
theaters.) Seen in this light, the play becomes a bleak
allegory of the present impasse on both fronts, with intimidation instead of cooperation from the manage-
ment/university authorities (the guardian) and servility
instead of self-determination from the labor force/stu-
dent body (the ward). This interpretation clearly in-
volves a reassessment of Handke's assertion that "It
would be repugnant to me to twist my criticism of a
social order into a story or to aestheticize it into a
poem." Insofar as his audience has not on the whole
discovered his political parable, he has kept to the letter
of his credo, though not to its spirit. It remains to be
seen whether he can continue so to abstract political
issues in his plays that they remain concealed from the
audience.

The impact of *My Foot My Tutor* cannot afford to
depend on such concealed allegories. More powerful
are the effects that work without the need of a key
to reveal them, such as the way that an action in one
scene will seem to be a distorted repetition of action in
an earlier scene. The somber variation on the coffeemaking scene has already been mentioned. Equally disturbing is the apparent connection between the guardian screwing his newspaper up into a ball and the ward
screwing himself into a little heap on the floor. Similarly
the almost frivolous scene where the ward throws burrs
at the guardian is soon countered by the more menacing
scene where the guardian throws crockery at the ward.
The effectiveness of these parallel actions and of other

suggestive moments cannot be explained intellectually: they must jolt the spectator's sensibility as does a ritual dance whose meaning is sensed but not deduced. Playgoers familiar with Pinter will have little difficulty with these rituals of intrusion and menace, domination and subservience, played out in the most effective *theatrical* terms with little regard for logic or probability. It doesn't matter *why* McCann is tearing off strips of newspaper in Act Two of *The Birthday Party*, and it never is explained—it is simply right in that situation.

If the use of semiritual enhances the play's ambiguity, so do the deliberate references to established theatrical and subtheatrical phenomena. As was Kaspar, both figures in *My Foot My Tutor* are reminiscent of traditional circus clowns going through their routines in poker-faced silence; they throw things at each other, they climb about on chairs and tables, they have business with hoses, and there is even the "inexhaustible pocket" routine, as the ward takes three apples, a book, a pencil, and several handfuls of burrs all out of the same pocket.

Even more are they reminiscent of the slapstick comics of the silent screen. For a start, the endless contest between the put-upon "little man" and the bullying "big guy" is the stock-in-trade of silent comedy plots; moreover, there is about the ward more than a little of the mute appeal of the stone-faced Keaton, incompetent but ever willing, going into battle against impossible odds, but maintaining his self-esteem and the audience's sympathy with flashes of foolish bravery (throwing the burrs) or sudden, impossible flukes (catching the plate); and in Peymann's production, the guardian's natural affinity to the silent "heavy" (usually Joe Roberts in Keaton films) was emphasized by casting him as a big

man complete with false paunch. A number of the
jokes, too, are borrowed from silent comedy routines:
at one point, the ward is following the guardian so
closely that when he stops, the ward bangs into him;
variations on the cat-flap joke turn up in Keaton's *The
Goat* and again in *The Scarecrow*; and when the ward
is caught by the guardian drawing in the book, he dith-
ers à la Harry Langdon, pretending that really he was
doing something quite different. Ultimately, the whole
play is built with the bricks of silent film comedy: short
scenes faded in and out, a setting full of fruitful possibilities, mimed action involving two men, and, of course,
musical accompaniment.

Equally striking are the direct references to characters and situations in the plays of Samuel Beckett, a
device that Handke extended in his next play, *Radio
Play No. 2*, to include verbatim quotations (in English)
from Beckett's *Eh Joe*. This device probably stems from
the modern cinema (another of Handke's special inter-
ests) where Jean-Luc Godard set the fashion by insert-
ing into his own films lengthy passages from films by
admired directors. The quotations were not made for
the purpose of satire or pastiche but in an attempt to
enrich the fabric of the work into which the quotation
is woven. This is Handke's intention in his obsessive use
of Beckett's theatrical vocabulary. By using another author's vocabulary alongside his own, Handke wishes to
multiply the associations of ideas in the spectator's
mind. So, both the phrasing of the stage directions in
My Foot My Tutor and the whole idea of a mimed
stage play are meant to refer to Beckett's two *Acts without Words*. The idiosyncratic style of Beckett's stage
directions—a string of verbs without the subject repeated—is well shown in *Act without Words I*:

He looks at his hands, looks round for scissors, sees them, goes and picks them up, starts to trim his nails, stops, reflects, runs his finger along blade of scissors, goes and lays them on a small cube, turns aside, opens his collar, frees his neck and fingers it.

Handke has realized the advantages of this style, its precision and impersonality, for his own purposes.

Moreover, as well as having business with scissors and nail cutting in common with *Act without Words I*, *My Foot My Tutor* also shares climbing up and down on furniture and ropes hanging down from the roof. But it has ever more in common with *Endgame*: two male figures (Hamm and Clov), one dominant, the other subservient (a relationship Beckett himself had refined from Pozzo and Lucky in *Waiting for Godot*), performing seemingly endless rituals in a "bare interior," and freezing to immobility in moments of impasse.

Perhaps the most Beckettian image in the play is the final one: the ward interminably dropping sand into a tub of water. Sand is a powerful and recurrent symbol in Beckett's work, suggesting the smothering, sterile, immeasurable sameness of every moment of existence, as exemplified in this passage from *The Unnamable*:

The question may be asked, off the record, why time doesn't pass, doesn't pass, from you, why it piles up all about you, instant on instant, on all sides, deeper and deeper, thicker and thicker, your time, others' time, the time of the ancient dead and the dead yet unborn, why it buries you grain by grain neither dead nor alive, with no memory of anything, no hope of anything, no knowledge of anything, no history and no prospects, buried under the seconds, saying any old thing, your mouth full of sand.

Handke uses his image of sand in much the same way. The impression created by the final scene of *My Foot*

My Tutor is above all of futility and hopelessness—the futility of the ward's action reflecting the hopelessness of his position and the pointlessness of all endeavor to get out of it.

The bleakness of this ending is emphasized when set against Handke's original treatment of this subject in a tiny 350-word short story written in 1965 called *Eye-Witness Account*. This tells how a mentally retarded adolescent, having been taught by his guardian (Vormund) how to operate a turnip-topping machine, gets hold of the man and shoves his head into the machine. The half-wit brings the blade down again and again and again, gradually having to slow down and use alternate hands, until finally the head is fully severed from the guardian's body.

The gleeful sadism of this version goes a long way toward explaining the permanent sense of menace that pervades the play, and it is all credit to Handke that he achieved this without having to resort to the violence of his original. More important, by denying his audiences the cartharsis that such violence would have afforded, he has considerably strengthened their receptivity to the depressing sense of hopeless stalemate, which is what the play is primarily about.

7

ooo

Quodlibet

First impressions of *Quodlibet*—that it is a thin and labored one-dimensional practical joke, that, technically and thematically, it represents a step backward to *Offending the Audience*, and that its only justification is as a failed draft of an idea that eventually matures in *The Ride over Lake Constance*—are not dispelled on closer acquaintance. Onto a bare stage stroll, in any order they like, a general, a bishop, a university chancellor, a Knight Hospitaler, a student corps member, a Chicago gangster, a politician with two bodyguards, a pair of ballroom dancing contestants, a lady in a long evening dress, and a pants-suited woman with a poodle —all "figures of the world theater," says Handke. These ten men, three women, and a dog proceed to chat among themselves, moving around the stage at will, for, say, forty minutes (the performance time of the Basel première). What they say and to whom they say it is left largely up to them; the title of the play is, after all, "What You Please." Handke does, however, explain the object of the game and provides some suggestions as to how to play it.

The game is simply that, by judicious choice of words and orchestration of their voices and movements, the actors shall try to delude the audience into thinking that a series of innocent conversations on stage are in fact exclusively concerned with sex, politics, and violence, by feeding the audience only partial information and thereby enticing them to complete the context by making (false) assumptions. For example, a sequence of quite innocent sentences from which the audience hears clearly only the words "gold tooth," "loading ramp," "electrified fence," "German sheep dog," "shoes," "tufts of hair," "towers," and "soap" will have the cumulative effect of leading the audience to think the conversation must be about concentration camps. Similarly, once a (false) context has been suggested, the audience can be made to hear certain signal words when other words with similar sound values are used: *"Ausschwitzen"* (to sweat) will be heard as "Auschwitz." Again, a number of words with two meanings, one harmless, the other less so, can be incorporated in their harmless sense into a succession of sentences until their very profusion misleads the audience into taking the wrong meaning. And so on. Handke's considerable ingenuity is taxed to the full in furnishing a suite of such examples. But to what purpose? Apparently to demonstrate an elementary precept of the psychology of perception: that what is said is not necessarily what is heard, and, further, that what is heard is not the same as what is understood. From which the not very startling deduction can be made that language is a fragile and often treacherous means of communication.

Since the implications of this idea were thoroughly investigated in *Kaspar*, *Quodlibet* can make no claim to originality of theme. And the trouble with the admittedly novel presentation is that it is so elaborate it runs the risk of misfiring altogether. The play is difficult enough to perform anyway, with the whole ensemble needing to achieve a precise modulation between clarity and indistinctness; and yet the more efficiently it is performed, the more even will be the texture, and the more likely the audience is to get bored and give up playing the game altogether.

One of the incidental felicities of the play is, in fact, Handke's plan of campaign for dealing with an audience grown restive. First he offers his actors a selection of the phrases that "politicians have ready for hecklers" and that are "therefore usable in case of heckling

from the audience." And if anyone attempts to invade
the stage (Handke is by now a veteran of riots at his
plays), the two bodyguards are to discourage him gently
but firmly.

Only toward the end, as the individual figures become increasingly self-absorbed, does the play seem to
shake off its monotony and become aware of the latent
surrealism in its bizarre collection of dramatis personae.
There is much mention of dreams; one of the women
lifts her dress revealing (symbolically, thought one
critic) that she has nothing on underneath; the light
grows dimmer; the figures gradually stop talking; the
bodyguards exchange obscene signs; the woman with
the dog utters a long-drawn-out sigh. . . . For all it is
probably intended, like the end of *Kaspar*, to convey the
disintegration caused by the treacheries of language,
the irrationality of this ending has a haunting quality
that transcends the rigors of the play's main theme and
intriguingly adumbrates the dreamlike atmosphere of
Handke's next play.

8

○○○

The Ride

over

Lake

Constance

Handke's second full-length play is a critic's dream in that, while clearly reusing certain elements from the author's earlier plays, it equally clearly represents an advance on these plays; but it is also a critic's nightmare in that this advance is into territory almost totally devoid of those landmarks, such as logic, consistency, sequentiality, by which a critic would normally find his way. Indeed, nightmare, or dream, is an apt description of the play, by far the most surreal of Handke's creations and reminiscent no longer of the abstract austerity of Beckett but rather of the cruel luxuriance of recent Luis Bunuel (*The Exterminating Angel, Belle de Jour*) or of the baroque inventions of the neglected Polish dramatist, Witold Gombrowicz. Talking in interview about his play, *The Marriage* (produced in Berlin in 1968, the first of a series of Gombrowicz productions in German theaters), Gombrowicz called it "obscure and dreamlike and fantastical: because it is so full of shadows, I wouldn't know how to analyze it fully myself. . . . Like all my works [it is] a revolt against form, a travesty of form, a parody of 'great drama.'" These words could well apply to *The Ride over Lake Constance*.

But, considering the persistence with which Handke has hitherto pursued his preoccupations, he is unlikely to have forsaken them merely for the decorative externals of surrealism. For a start, the new play is full of reminders of previous works. Thus, the five main characters (facetiously identified for the reader with the names of famous German stage and screen personalities of the 1920s) all look like refugees from the cast of *Quodlibet*. They do have a set this time, though, which looks like an amalgam of musical comedy and drawing-room drama—"Chekhov's *Cherry Orchard* transported to Hollywood," wrote the critic of *Die Zeit*. Their costumes are similarly nonspecific, although definitely theatrical—"intimations" rather than recognizable costumes. Like the figures in *Quodlibet*, they also indulge in apparently aimless conversation, but every word, every gesture is carefully laid down. And as at the end of *Quodlibet*, these characters too seem often more asleep than awake, and they too fall prey to an unmistakably insidious silence and inaction, somehow connected with a large, very lifelike doll, which is carried on by the black-faced woman who opens the play by vacuuming the room and removing the dust covers from the furniture.

Again, two of the characters, called Emil Jannings and Heinrich George, are locked in the dominant/subservient relationship familiar from *My Foot My Tutor*. But the other three, Elisabeth Bergner, Erich von Stroheim, and Henny Porten, seem caught up in a distorted eternal triangle: this, and their interaction with the first two, are new elements.

Again, there are a number of speeches in the play that are counterparts to "poems" in *The Inner World of the Outer World of the Inner World*. Particularly striking is the similarity between No. 20, *Mistakes* (*Verwechselungen*), where perfectly ordinary phenomena are misinterpreted as horrifying (a plane with its loading doors open is seen as a hungry shark on the runway), and Jannings's account of a "bad day" full of similarly disturbing mistakes (a "madwoman" trampling on eggshells is in fact breaking them up for the birds). Both the play and the suite of "poems" consistently reject the orthodox *outward* expression of *inner* thoughts and feelings, in favor of a more real and disturbing *inner world* normally kept repressed and submerged.

At this point, the play's relationship to *Kaspar* also begins to emerge. There are several devices in the new play that Handke first used in *Kaspar*; for instance when Elisabeth lapses into schizophrenia following an encounter with her reflection, and Henny restores her self-integration by reciting a number of syntactically identical sentences until Elisabeth is induced to imitate the model with an example of her own; or when Jannings kicks George at the precise moment that Stroheim kicks Henny, and Elisabeth delivers a paean in praise of order and coordination. But also in *Kaspar* there were hints of the terrifying abyss beneath the superficial semblance of order and linguistic competence. And it is this abyss, this innermost world beneath a thin veneer of normality, that opens up beneath our feet when we take *The Ride over Lake Constance*.

The title refers to a short ballad, *Der Reiter und der Bodensee*, by the Swabian poet Gustav Schwab (1792–1850), which tells of a horseman who, without knowing it, rides across the frozen Lake Constance but dies of fright when he learns of the danger he was in. The analogy with the thin ice of rationality on which we are all skating is exact; and it is essential we remain unaware of how thin the ice is if we are not to disintegrate with shock. In the words of Botho Strauss in *Theater Heute*:

The ride parallels the functioning of our grammar, of our system of coordinating perception and meaning, and of our linguistic and sentient powers of reason; it is only a provisional, permeable order, which, particularly when, as in Handke's play, it becomes conscious of its own existence, is threatened by somnambulism, schizophrenia, and madness.

The question remains, however, whether what is

called madness might not be preferable to accepted normality, just as Kaspar's original uncoordinated innocence seemed preferable to the social coordinate he became. The answer is given by the Kessler twins, who make a brief appearance toward the end of the play. Their identical appearance in ordinary .(untheatrical) clothes, looking as if they had "come into the production by mistake," their banal conversation ("How do you do? . . . Good day. . . . What time is it?"), their symmetrical movements, and their brisk tidying of the set, all mark them out as representatives of the orderliness of normality. But how dispiriting their normality is made to seem, and how easily it is seen to disintegrate as the twins leave the stage in confusion.

Botho Strauss sees in one of Henny's dreamlike speeches "about water and madness, and the Ships of Fools on the great rivers" a reference to Michel Foucault's treatise on *Madness and Civilization* (1961). Much more important than this single point of contact is the relevance Foucault's thesis has for the play as a whole. In attempting to define historically the "moment of conspiracy" when the thin ice dividing Reason and Madness first froze over, "Foucault makes it quite clear," says the Introduction to the English edition,

that the invention of madness as a disease is in fact nothing less than a peculiar disease of our civilization. We choose to conjure up this disease in order to evade a certain moment of our own existence—the moment of disturbance, of penetrating vision into the depths of ourselves.

And Foucault himself writes:

The constitution of madness as a mental illness, at the end of the eighteenth century, affords the evidence of a broken dialogue, posits the separation as already effected, and thrusts into oblivion all those stammered, imperfect words without fixed syntax in which the exchange between madness and reason was made.

In *The Ride over Lake Constance* Handke is concerned with reestablishing that broken dialogue, to question the assumptions "by which men, in an act of sovereign reason, confine their neighbors, and communicate and recognize each other through the merciless language of nonmadness" (Foucault), and to reinstate the ancient belief that madness is an expression of "the secret powers of the world." Handke has moved from a Wittgensteinian distrust of language to a Foucaultian distrust of what our society calls reason. His play is by no means surrealist in externals only: it parallels the surrealists' cardinal desire—the liberation of men's minds from the constraints of reason.

Thus Handke continues to demonstrate that the consistently *anti*-theatrical stance that he has maintained throughout his dramatic writing can nonetheless lend concrete theatrical expression to abstract philosophical ideas, thereby generating a new and valid form of theater.

○○○

First

Performances

In German

Publikumsbeschimpfung (Offending the Audience): 8
June 1966 at Theater am Turm, Frankfurt (director:
Claus Peymann), in context of Experimenta I.

Weissagung (Prophecy) and *Selbstbezichtigung* (Self-
Accusation): 22 October 1966 in double-bill at Stä-
dtische Bühnen, Oberhausen (director: Günther
Büch).

Hilferufe (Cries for Help): 12 September 1967 in Stockholm by actors from the Städtische Bühnen, Oberhausen (director: Günther Büch), in context of
German-Swedish Theater Week. Subsequently in
Oberhausen on 14 October 1967.

Kaspar: 11 May 1968 simultaneously at Theater am Turm,
Frankfurt (director: Claus Peymann; with Wolf R.
Redl as Kaspar), and at Städtische Bühnen, Oberhausen (director: Günther Büch; with Ulrich Wild-
gruber as Kaspar).

Das Mündel will Vormund sein (My Foot My Tutor):

31 January 1969 at Theater am Turm, Frankfurt (director: Claus Peymann).

Quodlibet: 24 January 1970 at Basler Theater, Basel (director: Hans Hollmann).

Der Ritt über den Bodensee (The Ride over Lake Constance): 23 January 1971 at Schaubühne am Halleschen Ufer, Berlin (directors: Claus Peymann, Wolfgang Wiens).

In English

Self-Accusation: broadcast in May 1968 on BBC Radio 3 (producer: Martin Esslin).

Offending the Audience: 24 December 1970 by The Other Company at Oval House, Kensington (director: Naftali Yavin).

Self-Accusation and *My Foot My Tutor*: 27 April 1971 by the Chelsea Theater Center of Brooklyn at the Brooklyn Academy of Music, New York (director: Wieland Schulz-Keil).

My Foot My Tutor: 29 September 1971 at Open Space Theatre, London (director: Ronald Hayman).

The Ride across Lake Constance: 13 January 1972 at the Forum Theater, Lincoln Center, New York (director: Carl Weber).

Kaspar: Forthcoming (director: Peter Brook).

○○

Bibliography

Works by Handke

(NOTE: All German titles are published by Suhrkamp Verlag, Frankfurt on the Main, except where stated otherwise.)

1. STAGE PLAYS

Publikumsbeschimpfung, und andere Sprechstücke (also includes *Weissagung* and *Selbstbezichtigung*). 1966.

Hilferufe. In: Karlheinz Braun, ed. *Deutsches Theater der Gegenwart 2.* 1967.

Kaspar. 1968. Also in: *Theater Heute* 9, no. 13 (1968).

Das Mündel will Vormund sein. In: *Theater Heute* 10, no. 2 (February 1969).

Quodlibet. In: *Theater Heute* 11, no. 3 (March 1970). Also in: *Spectaculum* 13 (1970).

Der Ritt über den Bodensee. 1971. Also in: *Theater Heute* 11, no. 10 (October 1970). And in: *Spectaculum* 14 (1971).

2. RADIO PLAYS

Wind und Meer (includes title play and *Hörspiel, Hörspiel Nr. 2*, and *Geräusch eines Geräusches*). 1970.

Hörspiel Nr. 2, 3, und 4. Frankfurt on the Main: Verlag
der Autoren, 1970.

3.   TV PLAY

Chronik der laufenden Ereignisse. Frankfurt on the Main:
Verlag der Autoren, 1970.

4.   FICTION

Die Hornissen. 1966.

Der Hausierer. 1967.

Begrüßung des Aufsichtsrats. Salzburg: Residenz Verlag,
1967.

Die Angst des Tormanns beim Elfmeter. 1970.

5.   POETRY

Die Innenwelt der Außenwelt der Innenwelt. 1969.

Deutsche Gedichte. Frankfurt: euphorion, 1969.

6.   ESSAYS AND SPEECHES

"Manifest" and "Zur *Publikumsbeschimpfung.*" *Spectaculum* 10 (1967):310–11.

"Briefe über Theater (1)." *Theater Heute* 8, no. 2 (February 1967):37.

"Wenn ich schreibe." *Akzente* 13, no. 5 (1967):467.

"Rede zur Verleihung des Gerhart-Hauptmann-Preises."
Theater Heute 11, no. 1 (January 1968):35.

"Horváth ist besser." *Theater Heute* 9, no. 3 (March
1968):28. Also in: Henning Rischbieter, ed. *Theater
im Umbruch.* Velber: Friedrich Verlag, 1970. pp.
62–63.

"Totgeborene Sätze." *Die Zeit,* 6 December 1968.

"Natur ist Dramaturgie." *Die Zeit,* 30 May 1969.

"Die Dramaturgie zweiter Teil." *Die Zeit,* 13 June 1969.

"Die Tautologien der Justiz." In: Michael Krüger and Klaus Wagenbach, eds. *Tintenfisch 3.* Berlin: Klaus Wagenbach Verlag, 1970. pp. 58–63.

"Nachbemerkung zu *Quodlibet.*" *Theater Heute* 11, no. 4 (April 1970):47.

7. COLLECTED EDITIONS

Der Gewöhnliche Schrecken. Neue Horrorgeschichten. Salzburg: Residenz Verlag, 1969.

Peter Handke: Prosa Gedichte Theaterstücke Hörspiel Aufsätze. 1969.

8. INTERVIEW

"Peter Handke." In: Artur Joseph. *Theater unter vier Augen.* Berlin: Kiepenheuer und Witsch, 1969. pp. 27–39.

9. IN ENGLISH TRANSLATION

Kaspar, and Other Plays (also includes *Offending the Audience* and *Self-Accusation*). New York: Farrar, Straus and Giroux, 1969.

Self-Accusation. In: Martin Esslin, ed. *New Theatre of Europe,* vol. 4. New York: Dell, 1970.

My Foot My Tutor and *Calling for Help* (also translated extract from interview with Artur Joseph). In: *Tulane Drama Review* 15, no. 1 (January 1971):57–87.

"Brecht, Play, Theatre, Agitation." *Theatre Quarterly* 1, no. 4 (October–December 1971).

102   *Peter Handke*

Offending the Audience, and Self-Accusation. London: Methuen, 1971.

Kaspar. London: Methuen, 1972.

The Ride across Lake Constance, translated by Michael Roloff. In: Michael Roloff, ed. *Contemporary German Drama.* New York: Avon Books, 1972.

Works about Handke

"Man, the Plaything of Language." *Times Literary Supplement.* 7 August 1970, p. 868.

Appenzeller, Heinz. "Sprachverhör und Verhörssprache: Peter Handkes Werke und Wirklichkeit." *Schweizer Rundschau* 69 (1970):57–60.

Blöcker, Günther. "Peter Handkes Entdeckungen." *Merkur* 21, no. 236 (1967): 1090–94.

Esslin, Martin. "Drama in Europe—New Writing. No. 2: Austria." *Plays and Players* 18, no. 8 (May 1971):20–21, 28.

Heißenbüttel, Helmut. "Peter Handke and His Writings." *Universitas* (Wayne State) 12, no. 3 (1970):243–51.

Hinck, Walter. "Von Brecht zu Handke—Deutsche Dramatik der sechziger Jahre." *Universitas* (Stuttgart) 24 (1969):289–301.

Kesting, Marianne. *Panorama des zeitgenössischen Theaters—58 literarischen Porträts.* 2d rev. ed. Munich: Piper, 1969.

———. "The Social World as Platitude." *Dimension* 2 (1969):177–81.

Lettau, Reinhard, ed. *Die Gruppe 47,* pp. 222, 233, 240, 244–45, 403–404, 436. Neuwied: Luchterhand, 1967.

Lind, Jakov. "*Die Hornissen*—zarte Seelen, trockene Texte." *Der Spiegel* 20, no. 29 (11 July 1969):79.

Neugroschel, Joachim. "The Theater as Insult." *American-German Review* 33 (1967):27–30.

Strauss, Botho. "Versuch, ästhetische und politische Ereignisse zusammenzudenken—neues Theater 1967–70." *Theater Heute* 11, no. 10 (October 1970):61–68.

Taëni, Rainer. "Handke und das politische Theater." *Neue Rundschau* 81, no. 1 (1970):158–69.

Vanderath, Johannes. "Peter Handkes *Publikumsbeschimpfung*: Ende des aristotelischen Theaters?" *German Quarterly* 43, no. 2 (March 1970):317–26.

Wendt, Ernst. "Der Behringer der Beat-Generation." *Theater Heute* 8, no. 8 (August 1967):6–8.

Werth, Wolfgang. "Handke von Handke." *Der Monat*, no. 250 (July 1969), pp. 97–101.

Index